Bedside Manners

Bedside Manners

A Practical Guide to Visiting the Ill

Katie Maxwell

Foreword by
Ronald H. Sunderland

 **BAKER BOOK HOUSE**
Grand Rapids, Michigan 49516

ISBN: 0-8010-6265-9

Fifth printing, September 1995

Printed in the United States of America

Illustrations by Sandy Wenell Thornton

Contents

Foreword

During the past decade, there has been a flood of pastoral aids for clergy and lay pastoral caregivers. Many suggestions have focused on authors' theological statements about ministry, some have given formats for the implementation of lay pastoral care programs, and still others have presented practical aids to shape pastoral ministry as a day-to-day function of the congregation. Katie Maxwell's book falls into the third category. Her work is filled with practical directions for offering pastoral care in a variety of settings: hospitals, the homes of shut-ins, and nursing homes. She addresses a concern which few have focused: the pastoral care of children. But she addresses also visits with dying patients, and care for the caregiver. Her book opens with "be-attitudes" of visiting, and closes with reflections on the church's role in pastoral visitation.

Lest the reader too quickly pass over *Bedside Manners* as merely just another "how to" book, let me be quick to commend it for further study. It is a book about the practice of pastoral ministry. The author displays a vivid grasp of the anguish of hospitalization and the basic pastoral responses to patients' anxieties. The reader is reminded of simple but basic characteristics of pastoral visitation: people need to know that there are people who care for them; visitation requires practice and patience; a visit is a time for compassionate caring, rather than an opportunity to teach some theological awareness, or even fulfil a "missionary" role.

The "be-attitudes" section offers a novel framework for introduction of practical steps to remember during visits: being prepared, learning how to be present, open, sensitive, and, importantly, "still," that is, learning to listen. Readers are reminded that they are to be there for the other person, rather than to meet their own needs. Introduction to visits to members in hospitals is accompanied by lists of dos and don'ts—the practical lessons that all pastoral visitors so easily take for granted. This section will be of particular value to beginning visitors. It concludes with a reminder that patients tend to be forgotten on discharge from the hospital, though they in fact still need support and ministry. The following sections, visiting shut-ins and nursing-home residents, are modeled after the early chapters, and are similarly replete with practical suggestions for the shaping of ministry.

The chapter on pastoral care of children will be of particular relevance to both clergy and lay caregivers. As I speak to clergy groups across the United States, I have become painfully aware that few clergy feel competent to minister to children. They confess that they lack training and often their sense of awkwardness inhibits them from initiating pastoral conversations. This means that children are forgotten, usually overlooked, by pastoral caregivers. The chapter identifies in a simple, straightforward manner the differences in developmental stages and pastoral measures appropriate to each stage. The strength of the section lies, once again, in a practical guide laced with more dos and don'ts. We are reminded that adults have much to learn from children, if only we will let them be our teachers.

The chapter on ministry with people who are dying begins, appropriately, with a sketch of the so-called "stages of grief," as a basis for understanding the needs of terminally ill people. I find it more helpful to avoid the term *stages*, and turn to identifying the "tasks" of mourning, and clarifying the "hard work" which the dying and their loved ones must undertake as the separation occasioned by death becomes imminent. The author's delineation of grief ministry is apt, and extends to simple, moving suggestions if the visitor is with the patient at the point of death.

Caregivers fall into two categories: the primary caregiver, that is, the family member responsible for day-to-day care, and the occasional caregiver, that pastoral caller who represents the congregation's ministry. The needs of the former are addressed in the short section "Helping the Primary Caregiver." The latter issue is discussed in the longer final chapter, where she sets lay pastoral ministry, training of lay caregivers, and the supportive role of oversight, or supervision, within the congregation's life as one of its fundamental functions. Pastoral caregivers are members called by the congregation to support the membership through supportive care and mutual ministry.

Bedside Manners is a practical guide to congregational pastoral care. It is a simple guide from which the beginning caregiver will benefit, but one which experienced caregivers can study to advantage. But it is more. It is a devotional book, for the reader is invited to pause and meditate on the place of prayer in both the life of the person visited, as well as in the life of the minister. It is a book to be pondered over, a book to be kept on the bedside table, or on the bookstand by your favorite chair, so that it can be picked up and read, a page or two at a time, until its lessons are part of the way you think about ministry.

Ronald H. Sunderland

Preface

One of the most rewarding ministries in which I have ever been involved began at American River Hospital in Carmichael, California. Under the supervision of Chaplain Christine Powell-Millar, I became a pastoral visitor.

Simply put, I visit people who are hospitalized. It didn't take long before I realized the important role visitors play in the life of a patient, and the way this opportunity has been a gift to me.

Unfortunately many people don't feel at ease around those who are ill. Because of this they tend to cut themselves off from sick persons at a critical time, when their support and friendship are needed most.

Bedside Manners is a book filled with practical information to help you through the visiting process. It will offer you the confidence you need to go beyond your comfort zone and help those who need your presence.

The information, ideas, and hints come from chaplains, nurses, lay visitors, and especially from the patients themselves. All have contributed ideas to make your visiting more helpful.

To be confident in the visiting ministry you must begin with prayer, feed on information, and then act on faith. *Bedside Manners* will supply you with the knowledge you need to be successful in this exciting and fulfilling work.

To the many people who watched and nurtured the growing of this book, I give my heartfelt thanks. To the nurses and patients who readily gave me input, I thank you for your time and honesty. A special thanks to Chaplains Ron Mulles, Patrick Thornton, Lowell Graves, Timothy Little, and Christine Powell-Millar, whose encouragement and knowledge made the project a reality. Peggy Gulshen deserves a special thanks for sharing her vast knowledge on working with children. I am also grateful to Pastor Steve Smith and to my dear friend Jerry Mountjoy for their editing skills. Thanks to Pastors Ken Working and Cliff Graves for their contributions.

And without the support of a loving husband and tolerant children, the idea would still be only floating in my head. Thank you, Michael, Holly, Justin, and Noah for letting me do this.

1

The BE Attitudes of Visiting

For I was sick . . . and you visited me. . . . When you did it to these my brothers you were doing it to me! (Matt. 25:36, 40 The Living Bible).

Illness is a physical, emotional, and spiritual crisis. It affects not only the person who is ill or injured, but also all of those associated with the patient. During times of crisis, persons may either grow from the experience or suffer as a result of it. Your response to the hurting patient during this time of crisis may determine the direction chosen.

You can walk alongside, not trying to fix their pain, but rather trying instead to comfort. Cancer victim Alden Sproull said, "Those who minister become co-sojourners in the most intimate, challenging experiences of life." When you visit those who are ill, you are communicating your concern by giving them the message that they are not alone.

We need to know that others care about us. Accompanying

a friend or loved one on this sometimes-frightening journey entails much more than just superficial conversation or
a cheering-up session. It requires the much deeper responsibility of relating to their anxieties, fears, and hopes.

Visitation takes practice and patience. Yes, it is true that
some people seem to have an inborn knack for helping
others, but our abilities, no matter how slight, can be
enhanced through awareness, education, and participation. All of us can develop our skills in this area to help
those who are hurting.

Visitation with the sick is *not* a time for proselytizing,
and as comforters, you should not make the patient's bedroom a missionary field. Being able to distinguish between
the spiritual and the religious is essential to effective comforting of the sick.

As visitors, the concern is for the spiritual well-being of
the patient. This deals with the personal, inner experiences
of life. Being able to enter the patient's world and respond
with feeling is the goal. Letting people express their fears
about their illnesses and walking with them as they question God's purpose is a spiritual journey.

Religion on the other hand looks more at the outward
expression of those spiritual beliefs. Giving the patient
communion is a religious function. While doctrine and
dogma may be important to the patient and definitely
have a place in the visit, it should not be the major empha-
sis. Searching out the deeply hidden spiritual concerns
should be the primary interest of the Christian visitor.

How Can You Do This?

Be prepared. Before your visit, take a moment to collect
your thoughts. It might be in your car in the parking lot. It
might be in the hospital chapel. Use these moments to shut
out the rest of the world. Center on your purpose for visiting. Pray. Pray that your presence will show the patient
that you are concerned and that God is concerned.

Be present. This doesn't mean just being in the same room. You need to be 100 percent there for that person. For the time you spend with the patient, that person is your most important concern—not forever, just for this moment. You may have to work at it. Don't be preoccupied with what you are going to do when you leave or what you did before you came. Be there with your complete concentration and attention.

Be open. Meet people where they are and in whatever mood you find them. Listen to what they have to say without being judgmental. They may have any number of emotions surfacing at the time of your visit—anger, frustration, fear, hopelessness. By not judging either through your words or body language, you are letting them feel safe to share with you. The moment you start to criticize or invalidate these genuine feelings, you are inviting withdrawal and insincere responses.

Be still. Listen, don't look for answers. Most people don't expect you to fix anything. They are looking for their own solutions and answers. They just need someone they can trust with their innermost thoughts to listen while they work it out for themselves. They will find their own answers if given the opportunity.

Be sensitive to their needs and condition. Read between the lines of what they are saying. Try to pick up on the underlying theme of their words. An example might be if the patient said, "I just don't want to be a burden to anyone." Your response might be, "Are you afraid that your illness is going to keep you from doing all of the things you used to do?" By asking open-ended questions such as this, you allow them to expand on the subject and share their fears and hopes.

(One patient that I worked with would always say, "I don't need you now, but maybe later." After the third time he concluded our visit with this statement, I asked, "What would have to happen for you to need me?" He responded by saying, "Well, if I found out I was going to die or something like that." This opened the door for me to ask, "Do you think that might happen?" Suddenly, our superficial exchange of niceties grew into a discussion about his fears of death.)

Be human. Admit that you don't have all of the answers. Say, "I don't understand why this is happening to you either." Tell them that *you* have fears and doubts sometimes too. Identify with their feelings whenever you can. This does not mean saying, "I know just how you feel." Because we are all different people with different histories, it is impossible for any of us to know just how another feels. But it is legitimate to say, "I've felt abandoned by God myself before."

Be supportive. As a visitor, your objective is to leave patients better than you find them. Try to leave them in a good place. Giving encouragement to those who are sick is one of the best ways we can help them.

Be silent. You don't have to fill in all of the silences with meaningless chatter. In some cases, you need not make conversation at all. Often when it becomes quiet, the patient begins to talk about what's really going on inside. Learn to be comfortable with these special silent moments. Holding a hand can communicate far more than any words ever could. The exceptions to the silent rule involve children or persons who are suffering from severe anxiety. Silence can be threatening to these folks. But mostly, let silence be your friend; just be there.

Be empathetic. "I'm here to travel with you wherever you need to go" is the message you want to convey. Visualize walking alongside and holding out a hand to support these patients should they stumble. Feel with them.

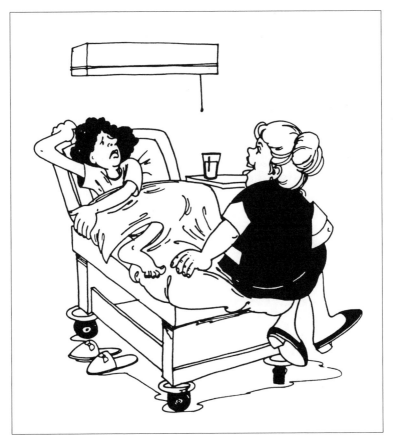

It's O.K. sweetie! I've cleared my calendar,
so I can stay right here all afternoon.

Identify by putting yourself in their situation. However maintain your objectivity so you can support the person.

Be compassionate. Convey that you care not only through your words, but also nonverbally through your willingness to sit close and touch. Have eye contact. Incline your ear in the patient's direction. Don't raise your eyebrows or frown when you hear something that you don't agree with. Tenderness and tolerance are important messages to convey.

Be yourself. The sick person has enough to deal with without having to figure out what's going on with you. Don't strain the relationship by being a stranger. Adapt who you are to the situation. As an example, there are times when humor is appreciated. If you have a natural sense for humor, share it at the appropriate time.

Be selfless. Be there for the patient's needs, not for your needs. The patient may not want what you have to offer at the moment you offer it. A lot of good intentions flounder at this point because the visitor wants to *do* something. Very often, the patient just needs someone to *be* rather than to do.

Ask what the patient needs and respond accordingly. Too often it is the visitors who need to clear their consciences. They seek the patient's forgiveness for past omissions or neglect. One patient told me that she never sees her son (who lives less than a mile from her) until she goes into the hospital. Then he comes and sits all day, keeping her from much needed rest.

Be positive. There are enough negative experiences going on around the patients. They need a positive attitude from their visitors. Delete negative words from your vocabulary. Stop thinking that a cancer diagnosis is a death sentence or that a stroke means the patient will never function independently again.

Be willing to get involved. Take risks. Give a part of yourself away to each one you visit.

Be respectful of the diverse beliefs of patients. This does not mean that you will make light of or ignore your own beliefs. It does mean that you will not cram them down the throats of those who happen not to agree. If this person is a friend, you will have other times to share your beliefs and opinions. This is not the time. If the person is only casually connected to you, trust that another at a better time will have the words and wisdom to share.

Be mindful of using Scripture appropriately. Don't use the reading of Scripture as a chance to be judgmental. Instead of condemning, the verses you share should be full of hope and encouragement. (*See* Appendix 1 for some suggestions.) Many patients will not have the stamina to listen to long readings, so choose a few short passages to share. Ask if the patient would like you to read from the Scriptures before you do. This may not be a comfortable time for the sufferer.

Be ready to pray when given permission to do so. Don't use this special time as an opportunity for a minisermon. It's tempting to ask the Lord for the things *we* want for the patient within earshot. Recap what you talked about. Ask if they have any specifics they want you to pray about. One patient wanted to live long enough to get her personal affairs in order. Another wanted to die a peaceful death. These are specific petitions that you can present to God for and with the patient.

Pray for the courage to cope, for understanding, and for acceptance of God's plan. Pray for strength for the family and loved ones. Pray that the medical team will have the knowledge and compassion to do the best job that they can. Pray for peace and calmness and healing for the emotions, the spirit, and the body. Give thanks.

Jesus' Example

Jesus' encounter with the Samaritan woman at the well in the fourth chapter of John, gives us a perfect formula for relating to all persons whether sick or not. First, out of love for all mankind, Jesus goes to Samaria where he speaks to a woman drawing water from a well. He accepts her where she is and as she is. He doesn't shun her because she is a "despised" Samaritan. Next, through his conversation and nonthreatening body language, he gains her trust. He then listens to what she has to say. He doesn't let her past interfere with his compassion. He offers encouragement by way of sharing the truth about who he is. Her response is then up to her. She may either accept or reject his offer.

This pattern is repeated throughout Jesus' dealings with people in all walks of life. It bears imitation: *going, accepting, gaining trust, listening, offering encouragement, showing respect,* and then *leaving the response up to the patient.*

In contrast read the story of Job to find out how not to respond. When three of Job's friends first heard of his tragedy, the Bible says they "set out from their homes and met together by agreement to go and sympathize with him and comfort him" (2:11).

They demonstrated their sorrow and sat with him in silence for seven days, never speaking a word. So far, so good—but then Job begins to lament his birth, and one of the friends asks to put in his two cents. He accuses Job of having sinned and advises him to confess and ask God's forgiveness so that he can be delivered.

The second friend asks, "How long will you say such things? Your words are a blustering wind" (8:2). He tells Job that if he were so pure and innocent, these things wouldn't be happening to him.

As Job becomes more frustrated and discouraged, his third friend accelerates his condemnation. Like the others, he continues to hound Job and accuse him of all sorts of false pride. Job pleads with the friends to be silent, but they continue to taunt him. Job finally tells the three, "miserable comforters are you all!" (16:2).

In looking over the BE Attitudes, it is easy to see how Job's friends could have been more helpful. It is easy to find ourselves unwittingly imitating some of the same behaviors. Being aware of what is helpful and what is not can save the visitor from such criticism.

A Visitor's Prayer

Gracious Lord,
Beneath whose eye and within whose love the story of
    our lives is told;
Give me grace to pause in my hurried pace to bear
    your love and bring your grace to someone ill this
    day.

Let me listen without judgment, care without condi-
    tion, pray without ceasing;
Just tell me what to say.

Go before, walk beside, live within I pray.
I am ready, Lord, guide me in my way.
Amen.

Dr. Kenneth C. Working

2

Visiting in Hospitals

Visits from family and friends are an important part of our recovery, a magic medicine that lifts our spirits even when our heads lie heavy on the pillows (NORMA R. LARSON, Hospital Patience).

Hospitals can be rather scary places. It's like going into a foreign country where the language is different and the sights and smells are unfamiliar.

Imagine yourself a reliant, confident person who goes to the doctor because of some minor complaints that just won't go away. After an examination the doctor tells you to go across the street for some lab work. After dutifully giving blood and having Xrays, the technician tells you to go home and wait for the doctor to call with the results.

The waiting game begins. Two days later, the nurse from your doctor's office calls to tell you that the doctor would like further tests. You begin feeling a little anxious and ask, "Is there a problem?" The nurse gives some noncommittal answer and tells you where to go and what tests must be done.

The waiting game continues. The day after your second battery of tests, the nurse calls and says the doctor would like to see you in his office.

You nervously sit and wait for your name to be called. Finally, after what seems like hours, you are escorted to the doctor's office. "There seems to be a small growth on your lung. I'd like you to have surgery to see if we can remove it. How soon can you be at the hospital?"

All kinds of questions come to mind, but you are too shocked at the news to ask them. The last week of waiting has been emotionally tedious. You mumble something about Thursday being fine.

More waiting. Wednesday night before entering the hospital, your sleep is interrupted with bad dreams. You wake often and look at the clock. Thursday morning arrives.

Walking into the hospital, you immediately feel invasion of privacy as the person at the admittance desk asks personal questions regarding your age, marital status, number of children, religious affiliation, employer, insurance company, finances, next of kin, and countless other questions.

Then you are directed to a room where your clothes are hung in a small closet, and you are asked to put on a rather drab and immodest-looking gown. People, mostly strangers, come and go at will—theirs, not yours. Your body is invaded by needles and tubes. Hours before the surgery is scheduled, the doctor decides an additional test is needed. You wait for the tests. You wait for the test results. Seldom does any of this happen on schedule as planned.

In the meantime, you are sharing a room with one or more strangers who may be in pain and moaning. This adds a whole other dimension. They may want to talk when you feel like resting. They may watch television all night or play the radio too loudly. They may soil their beds often and foul the room with bad odors. Their visitors may come too often, too many, and be too loud.

Or you may be in a room all by yourself where there is no one with whom to talk or compare experiences. Feelings of isolation begin to creep in on you.

Surgery is delayed until the last test results can be studied. You eat when food is served rather than when you are hungry. Sometimes you are not allowed to eat at all. Your sleep is interrupted by nurses giving you pills, checking your blood pressure, taking your temperature, asking if you are asleep.

Visitors may be limited by certain hours or in certain numbers.

Your diet and fluid intake may be restricted. You may even be told when and how you can go to the bathroom.

There may be limited times when you can bathe or shower, and it is in a bathroom where the faucets look and feel odd.

The medical staff discusses your condition using words, terminology, and abbreviations that sound like a foreign language. Procedures are performed for purposes that you sometimes don't understand.

You begin to feel intimidated by the whole hospital atmosphere.

As you wait for the test results and the ensuing surgery, you begin to imagine the worst. What if you have to change your lifestyle? What if you lose a body part? Will your employer hold your job open if you have to be hospitalized for weeks? How will you pay all of your bills if you can't work? How will your spouse react? Who will take care of the kids? Will you need to go to a convalescent hospital afterward until you can manage at home?

Your future suddenly becomes uncertain. Fears and anxieties begin to take over that part of you that once was confident and steadfast. You are in crisis, as is your whole network of close family and friends.

While the above scenario may vary according to where the patient lives and the type of insurance the patient may or may not have, the feelings involved in hospitalization are very similar for most patients, no matter how many times they go into the hospital. Each visit has its unique set of circumstances that make the patient feel out of control.

Why Is Visiting Important?

In the hospital environment, the physical body in crisis is given the most attention. The medical field, perhaps as a result of societal acceptance, is gradually acknowledging the ramifications of the emotions in the healing and getting sick process. But the spiritual dimensions and implications are, for the most part, being neglected. It is in this area that the visitor can play a vital role in the total healing process.

Because the changes that are occurring are rapid and many, it is easy to understand why patients feel powerless. As a visitor, you have the ability to give them back a measure of control. By simply asking such questions as "Do you feel like visiting?" or "May I sit down?" or "Is this a good time to talk?" you are letting them direct the visiting situation. Rather than being just another person telling them what they must do, you are, by asking, allowing them to take control as they see fit.

Visitors let the patient know they are not alone. They can relieve that great sense of isolation that surrounds the patient.

Visitors who have an especially close relationship with the patient can act as patient advocates, making sure questions get answers and basic needs are met. Interceding for patients when they are too intimidated or too debilitated to fight their own battles is advocacy at its finest.

Not only can visitors give the patient encouragement, but they can also encourage the primary caregiver. Staying with the patient while the caregiver goes home to shower, eat or sleep, can be of great help.

Although not always the case, there may be occasions where visitors may extend their ministry to the person in the next bed, thus reaching out showing God's concern to others.

Being Sensitive to the Patient

Although visitors are usually a welcome relief from the boredom and isolation of the hospital room, be aware that the timing of your visit may not always be met with the enthusiasm you hoped for. The patient may be nauseated and unable to carry on a pleasant conversation. It may be taking every bit of their concentration to tolerate pain.

Because of medication, the patient may be drowsy or a little incoherent. They may be just plain grouchy because of the circumstances in which they find themselves. Visitors may have been dropping in all day, and they are tired of talking. Patients often find themselves ostensibly caring for the ones who come to visit. They may have no energy left to give to another visitor.

Men as well as women are often self-conscious about the way they look. One lady told me she didn't want any one from her church to know she was in the hospital because she couldn't bear for them to see her without her makeup and hair styled.

It may just be a wrong time for your visit. The patient may need to go to the bathroom, or have gas, or be sleepy.

Patients may be depressed or scared and find it difficult to carry on chitchat. It is not uncommon for patients to feel responsible for their own conditions. Often you will hear the smokers blame their habit for the lung cancer they now face. It is not your job to agree or disagree, merely to let them vent their feelings. Give them permission to verbalize their feelings of guilt, remorse, or responsibility for their illness without indicating that they are ill because they have sinned. While it is true that years of bad habits or neglect may result in illness, the patient should not be made to feel that the illness is punishment from God for personal sins.

Be careful not to expect patients to be a host or hostess. Although it is critical that you remember you are in their bedroom, whether that be in a hospital or at home, you should not expect them to play the role of server. Your function is to serve *them*, to meet *their* needs, not to have your needs met.

Finally, don't visit if you are not feeling well yourself. The immune system of the patient may be very low and unusually susceptible to your viruses. This is one unneeded complication. A phone-call visit would be much better in this case.

How Can You Help?

Often people are heard to say, "I don't know what to do," or "I don't know what to say," or "I don't know how I can be of help." Granted, visiting a sick friend can be tough. But fear of doing the "wrong" thing should never keep you from visiting. It's important that you maintain that relationship throughout an illness or injury. Sticking by a loved one during these times will result in a lot of personal growth for both of you.

The following list of *Dos* and *Don'ts* is a guideline to help you get an idea of the practical ways you can be helpful during your visits, keeping in mind that there are always delightful exceptions to every rule.

DO

Call first. Ask if they feel up to visitors and when a good time would be. They may have tests scheduled or be going to therapy. While calling first is ideal, it may not always be practical. When it is not possible, take your chances, but be ready to leave if circumstances warrant.

Visit before surgery. This is the time when they might feel most apprehensive and need a hand to hold and reassuring words. Patients need to feel confident about their surgeries. The minutes, hours, or days before surgery need to be filled with hope for a successful outcome that will promote healing. As a visitor, you can encourage these feelings.

Touch. One of the worst fears a patient has is being in isolation and not being able to have visitors. Part of the hospitalized's depression is caused by the fact no one can touch them. A gentle touch lets a patient know you care. A hug can do wonders for someone who is hurting emotionally. During one visit an elderly woman told me how her family was too busy to come and see her. She talked about how she wished her children were young again, when they used to run to her and give her hugs and kisses. My response was to ask her if I could give her a hug. She beamed and accepted my offer enthusiastically. (Be aware of IVs and other needles so that you don't hurt a tender spot!)

Take along your sense of humor. Laughter is said to be good medicine. Michael Duckworth, in the book *Funny Bones: Health and Humor Specialists* (Royal Publishing, Inc.), tells how his wife Carol clipped an appropriate cartoon from a magazine and gave it to him before his surgery. The cartoon kept resurfacing throughout his hospitalization—even on his chest where he taped it for the medical staff to see when they went into surgery.

Another patient wore big bear claw slippers a friend had given him. They were a source of pleasure for all who saw them.

One patient opened the bag her friend had helped her pack for her hospital stay to find a pair of those glasses with the big nose and moustache attached. It brought her a big smile at a nervous moment.

Slapstick comedy or making light of someone's fears is different and can be insensitive to someone in crisis. For instance, telling a joke about the "guy who died and Saint Peter wouldn't let him into heaven because . . . " would be very inappropriate for those who have recently been told they have a terminal illness.

Encouraging someone with humor is more like subtle permission to laugh at life even in the most tense times. Recalling a funny incident that happened in the hospital, something amusing a child said, or a funny movie plot can be a welcome relief to a weary soul.

Take your cues from the patient about how long you should stay. If they appear to be uncomfortable, sleepy, or in pain leave graciously. More frequent short visits are usually best. A visit of fifteen to twenty minutes is average.

Visit quietly out of consideration for the patient's roommates. This doesn't mean you need to whisper. A normal, controlled voice is acceptable.

Let them know that you are comfortable talking to them about sensitive subjects, including death. A terminally ill patient told me that she was so glad when I visited her because I was the only one that let her talk about death. Her friends and family would tell her that everything was going to be okay and not to talk "like that."

Keep any information shared with you confidential unless given permission to share with others. Your friend may tell you something that was meant to go no further. If it comes back in another form, your friend will be hesitant to share with you in the future.

Avoid offering false hopes. While you never want to remove all hope, keep that hope within the realm of reality.

Maintain comfortable eye contact. This usually means at or below their eye level. Don't make them strain or shift positions to see you or look into the light. Standing over patients, besides giving them a less than aesthetic view of your nostrils, can psychologically make them feel controlled. After all, you are above them, looking down at them.

Try to schedule your visits other than at mealtime. Eating in bed is awkward enough without trying to carry on a conversation with a mouthful. Ever try to eat when someone is staring at you? An exception to this is if the patient needs assistance in eating. Busy nurses will welcome your help if this is the case.

Excuse yourself when the doctor comes into the room (unless you have been asked by patients to stay and be a "second ear" to help them take notes, ask questions, and so forth).

Make pleasant conversation. What would you talk about if you were both sitting at the kitchen table?

Remind your friend of other personal battles won. Encourage the patient to draw on that inner strength. Convey the confidence that the present crisis too can be overcome. Assure the patient of your presence as pain and disappointment seem to dominate the day.

Get up-to-date information on the person's illness where possible. There are organizations that deal with almost every disease that can send you brochures (*see* Appendix 2). Many larger communities have self-help groups. Get a list of names and phone numbers. Hospital chaplains are often a good source of information. Much of a patient's anxiety is caused from a lack of adequate information about the illness. By reading the material yourself, you can be more understanding and helpful with the patient's questions and fears, but encourage the patient to get more information from the physician or have a family member do so.

Observe signs and notices on the patient's door. These are posted most often for the patient's protection and well-being. The immune systems may not be functioning properly or the patient may need rest. Double-check with the nurse in the event there has been a change that has not been posted. If the patient is in isolation, it may still be possible for you to put on the proper attire and visit. Ask the nurse for help and follow the hospital procedures.

Check with the nurse concerning mobility before you help the patients out of bed or take them for a walk. They may be restricted or need to be close by for scheduled procedures or monitoring, or considered "a high fall risk."

Be aware of the patient's diet before offering food or drink. An innocent drink of water may result in harm, if the patient is restricted to no fluid intake. Look for posted signs over the beds and check with the nurse first. A patient may not be fully aware of restrictions or may be tempted to "cheat" a bit with you as the unknowing accomplice.

Talk about the outside world. This helps to alleviate the feeling that the world is passing them by as they lie in bed. Heard any good jokes lately? Share them. Know any good news about mutual friends? Tell all.

Sit close. Standing across the room does not lend itself to intimate sharing and can make the patient feel contagious, even when that is not the case.

Knock and receive permission before you enter a room especially when the door is closed or a curtain is pulled. Often, the patient is sitting on the bed pan, being bathed, or is in some other way not suitable to receive visitors.

Be cheerful. A smile is often one of the most refreshing things a patient sees all day.

Brush patient's hair, do her nails, shave his stubble, shampoo her hair, help her apply her makeup, trim his beard, give her a massage. Of course you'll want the patient's permission and cooperation, but this can be a very valid way of making that person feel special. It's amazing how much better men and women feel when they are groomed!

Visit if you say you are going to. Keep your promises. Often patients lie and wait for that promised family member or friend who said they were coming, only to be sorely disappointed when the visitor doesn't show up. One patient told me how she forgoes taking pain medication when visitors are expected so that she can be alert.

Play games. I can remember my mother bringing the Scrabble game and playing with me. It passed a lot of boring hours. Just keep in mind the patient's condition and stamina.

My Aunt Mary, rest her soul, had the same surgery.

Make the patient feel needed. Telling the hospitalized that everything at home is just great without them may make them feel no longer useful. Ask for advice. Let patients know that things will be better when they are back home or in the office or church, and so forth.

Avoid addressing patient as "honey," "sweetie," and other such patronizing titles. Calling them names we would normally reserve for children has a way of making the patient feel more helpless. Mr. or Mrs. is more respectful for the elderly unless of course you are related or have been on a first-name basis prior to the visit.

Ask how you can help. There is a difference in saying, "Call me if I can do anything," and "How may I help you?" They are more apt to respond to the latter. For some, a direct "Can I go to the post office for you?" may be necessary.

Face the door when possible so that you are not tempted to turn around every time someone walks past the door or check out a strange sound.

Depending on hospital rules and the endurance and permission of the patient, bring children to visit. Well behaved, they can be a real breath of fresh air. If they will be seeing tubes and needles, prepare them ahead of time for what they will see, explaining that all of this "stuff" is helping the patient get better.

Avoid probing or rapid-fire questions. Inappropriate questions would be, "What are you in the hospital for?" or "What's wrong with you?" Although we may be curious about their surgery, illness, or treatment, if the patient doesn't introduce the subject it usually means they don't want to talk about it.

Think of your visit as a social visit, not something you are obligated to do. Maintain the image of hospitality. Share news about mutual friends. Originally hospital meant a place of shelter and rest where travelers received friendly and kind treatment.

Be sensitive about how you expose your own anxieties. Inappropriate "running on at the mouth," body language, or laughter at the wrong times is a giveaway.

Keep contact. Boredom and isolation are big issues for those who are hospitalized. A friend said that he got lots of visitors right after his surgery. It was several days later that he could have really enjoyed their visits more, but by then he was "old news."

Read to them, if they like. You might find an especially meaningful magazine story to share. Humorous stories would be great. Every opportunity to laugh is cherished. This does not mean you are going to try to cheer them up if they are feeling depressed. You are merely sharing some good things as well as the bad.

Let the patient cry. This includes men, too. Don't be embarrassed by tears. It may be appropriate to shed a few yourself as long as you don't become emotionally out of control and are no longer able to support the patient. If they start to apologize for "being such a baby" tell them how cleansing tears can be. Share with them how Jesus wept when he was sad. Tears are a very human and valuable commodity.

Affirm their loss whatever it may be. They could be grieving the loss of a lifestyle they will have to alter, or the loss of a body part, or the loss of independence or any number of other possibilities. Some losses may be temporary, while others may be permanent. Whichever the case, let them know that they have a right to grieve that loss and that you understand.

Offer to check on the patient's house, water the plants, feed the pets; or run any errands such as going to the cleaners, going to the post office, having the car serviced, and so forth.

Sit down and spend some quality time. You may have to go searching for a chair or drag one across the room. That's okay. If you remain standing, the patient will get the impression you are in a hurry to leave.

Focus the conversation on the patient, not on your problems. Follow the lead of the person you are visiting as to topics discussed and how much is shared with you. Let the patient direct what is going to happen. Remember, we visit by the consent of the patient. Therefore let the patient be in charge of the visit.

As a family member, ask the nurses questions if you don't understand something. One nurse said, "Try not to feel like you're in the nurse's way. Feel at home, you're not a pest." Consider yourself as a part of the healing team. You are!

Take a little surprise. Here are some ideas: magazines, books (inspirational, funny, instructional), silly wind-up toys (even for adults), stuffed animals, balloons, *TV Guide,* tapes (music or inspirational talks), flowers/plants, stationery with pen and stamps, food or drink (with nurse's approval), assorted teas, materials for knitting, crocheting, needlepoint, or cross-stitch projects, a basket filled with beauty items, pictures, church bulletin, organization newsletter, pocket maze, puzzles, hand mirror, personal-care items, cartoons, brain teasers, something that will remind them of a special time. One patient received a basket with several individually wrapped little gifts with instructions to unwrap one each day.

Offer to make phone calls, write notes, mail letters.

End the visit well. Don't make an excuse about why you

have to leave. Tell them how much you enjoyed seeing them and how you look forward to the next visit. Leave when they are feeling good about what has been going on so that you can pick up where you left off next visit.

Depend on the Lord to direct your visit.

DON'T

Let technology become a barrier to your visit. Tubes, machinery, and monitors that make beeps and diagrams can be very disconcerting. Focus on the fact that in spite of all this technology, what is really there is a person. It's easy to forget we have a human being somewhere in the midst of all of those wires and tubes.

Whisper when talking to the medical staff or family as if you don't want the patient to hear. This can be alarming and lead to misinterpretation on the part of the patient.

Sit on patient's bed. This can pull the covers tightly over the patient's feet; it can interfere with tubes; jiggling the bed can be very uncomfortable for the patient.

Sit on the empty bed next to patient. The nurse will have to remake the bed. This takes a lot of the staff's valuable time. Find a chair.

Break hospital rules. Observe visiting hours, age limits, or any other regulations established by the hospital.

Flatter the patient. Telling the sick that they look great when obviously they don't is insincere and not helpful. By the same token, giving honest feedback when you do see improvement can be encouraging.

Take their negativism personally. They may be angry, depressed, or just plain grouchy. This is a result of their fear and frustration and not a result of anything you did. Be patient. Their mood will improve.

Smoke or eat in the patient's room.

Tell your troubles to the patient. The hospitalized have enough to deal with already. Remember the focus should be on the sufferer's backache, not yours.

Show shock at odors, tubes, needles, and so forth. A dying student nurse wrote, "I sense your fright. And your fear enhances mine."

Watch television. Remember, you came to visit.

Get involved in family disputes.

Look at your watch. The patient will get the idea that you are in a hurry. Your message should be that the patient is more important than anything else you have to do.

Negate their feelings. If they say they feel like giving up, then help them to clarify those feelings. Affirm, don't moralize. Saying, "You shouldn't feel that way" is not productive.

Make promises you can't keep or offers you won't fulfill. By your following through, the patient will know that you are dependable.

Tell horror stories or compare illnesses.

Correct their answers or finish their stories. Let them do the talking. Give them time to answer.

Finish their sentences for them. It is so tempting to help someone who is struggling for the right word. Stroke victims are especially susceptible to someone "helping" them say what they want to say. It can be very humiliating for the patient.

Assume anything. Let them tell you how they feel and what is going on with them. Assuming that you already know interferes with listening.

An example is when you assume that a person is delighted about going home from the hospital. Sometimes the situation at home is dreadful or the person is afraid that the condition or ailment will take a turn for the worse, and help won't be available. It may be lonely at home.

This also applies to the patient's appearance. I have visited with patients in the evening who outwardly looked rather well only to find out the next morning that they died during the night. It is not uncommon for a patient's condition to appear to have improved just before death. Don't assume that there will always be another time for you to tell the patient the things you want to say to them.

Defend God or anyone else or anything.

Be judgmental. It's easy to be critical when you are feeling great. Avoid the use of words like *ought* and *should*. And don't use stories about people in similar situations to show your disapproval. While you may think it is a good way to get your point across, it is very transparent.

Criticize the doctor or the prescribed treatment. The patient needs to have confidence in both. But do encourage questioning the doctor if they feel unresolved about their condition or treatment.

Wake patient unless the nurse says it is okay, but leave a note that you stopped in.

Visit a patient the day after a major surgery. A recovering surgical patient is apt to be drowsy and in a lot of discomfort.

Try to cheer up patients when they really want to talk about how scared they are.

Use the word we *to talk about the patient.* "How are we doing?" or "Are we feeling better today?" not only sounds silly, but is very patronizing.

Recuperation Time

Once patients have left the hospital, it's easy to forget about them. Everyone assumes that since they are well enough to go home, they must be ready to resume a normal schedule.

Unless you have gone through a serious illness, you might not realize the length of time it takes to recuperate physically as well as emotionally from the experience. The visitor's support is needed as much or perhaps even more now that the person is home. It is important that you continue your calls, visits, and cards.

This is a time for you doers to mobilize your abilities. There are many things that can be done to show your love and concern. You could offer to cook a meal, drive the patient to follow-up doctors' visits, take over the car-pool duty for the mom, baby-sit, pick up prescriptions, mow lawns, clean house, grocery shop. Think of all of the errands you run during the day and offer to do your friend's at the same time.

Because patients don't like to impose, you may have to be a little assertive. "I'm going to the grocery store. What can I pick up for you while I'm there?"

Just saying, "Call me if you need anything," is not likely to get any response. Show the patient you really mean it.

A Hospital Visitor's Prayer

Dear God, we come to you with full hearts and minds. You know our concerns as you know and love each of us, but you also tell us to knock, seek, and ask . . . and so we do.

We give you thanks for all of the ways you have already blessed us, walked with us, loved us . . . and we depend on your promise to be with us always.

At this time we are especially asking that you be with this man (or woman) in a way that he can really sense your presence, feel your peace within him. He seeks your healing touch for his mind, body, and spirit.

We know you have a way of seeing things that we don't, and we are depending on your guidance and encouragement to keep moving on our paths in tune with your love and what you call us to do and be.

We need your challenge and comfort for today and the days to come.

We pray for all of the people in this place, be they patients, their families, friends, or staff. Each one needs your loving guidance and healing touch in particular ways. May this continue to be a hospitable place to your loving actions in our lives.

God, we thank you most of all for your gift of Jesus, your Son. We know the depth of your love in such a gift. He walked this earth, shared our joys and burdens in human life and walks with us now through the spirit.

It is in his name that we pray.

Amen.

CHRISTINE POWELL-MILLAR, CHAPLAIN

3

Visiting Shut-ins

Kindhearted humans can rally magnanimously at a deathbed, but they are not prone to rally to a person who can't manage either to get better or else die (KATHRYN LINDSKOOG—author, lecturer, and Multiple Sclerosis victim).

People with long-term or chronic illnesses often find themselves unable to leave their homes and participate in the activities they once enjoyed. They become prisoners in their own homes. It can be likened unto house arrest with the complications of just never feeling physically quite up to par.

Visitors become discouraged by the amount of time they will have to invest in these situations and often neglect shut-ins.

People who are ill for long periods of time find that their number of friends dwindles. Friends become bored or frustrated.

Shut-ins themselves begin to feel guilty about taking up

other people's time, so they gradually isolate themselves by not asking for help or company. Many would rather do without than impose on friends and acquaintances, even in their own churches.

In such a case, I was explaining to an elderly woman that I could not come over until 3:00 because I had to pick up my son at school that day. She interpreted that as my being too busy to come see her. Immediately she began saying, "Oh, don't bother. I don't want you to go out of your way. It's okay if you can't come today."

Because they are not likely to ask for help, shut-ins are easily and often forgotten. And without the care and nurture of people on the outside, they may vegetate when there still might be ways they can lead a productive life. You don't want to make invalids of persons who can do some things for themselves.

A primary goal for the visitor to shut-ins is to help them locate the resources available to enable them to be as active and productive as possible. This might be done through acquiring special equipment or services. Examples might be obtaining a microwave oven so that they can easily prepare their own meals; renting an electric wheelchair so that they have mobility around the house; contacting a meal service that will deliver meals to the house; having a housekeeper come in on a regular basis; or having special amplifiers installed on the telephones so that they can speak comfortably with others.

Whatever the plan, be sure that your aim is to support the shut-in's efforts to be as independent as possible. It is aligned with the philosophy "Give them a fish and they will eat today. Teach them to fish, and they will feed themselves tomorrow."

Once people see that there are things they *can* contribute, it gives them a sense of belonging. Although their positions might change, they can still play in the game. They begin to feel needed. Shut-ins may be an important link in the church prayer chain. They may be able to make some simple craft items for the church fund raiser. They may be able to be on a telephone committee. Perhaps they can stuff envelopes or fold bulletins.

It is important for them to feel like they are still a part of the congregation. I have heard the comment many, many times, "I don't have a church anymore. I used to be 'such and such' but my health got bad, and I haven't been able to go for a long time." Shut-ins who make these statements feel like they no longer belong to a church family, just when they need that love and support the most. How sad for everyone—the shut-in and the family of Christ.

At first shut-ins may be leery and full of excuses why they can't participate in anything anymore. Be persistent without being pushy. Keep going back and keep offering to help them explore the possibilities for their new circumstances. Help them regain control of their lives however you can. Be attentive to their needs. Ask the open-ended questions: "What are you worried about most?" or "How can I help you?" Then problem solve with them, making a plan of action, and then encouraging them to follow through.

There may be support groups with which you can put them in touch (*see* Appendix 2). These can be valuable in letting the confined person know that others have gone though similar circumstances. Make some phone calls and prepare a list of groups that might interest your shut-in.

Encourage them to keep learning. There is a wide variety of instructional video tapes available today that teach all sorts of things. If the shut-in cannot see well enough to read, books on audio cassettes are available on just about all subjects.

Encourage creative growth through art, music, writing, and crafts such as quilting, needlepoint, crocheting, knitting, wood carving, leather tooling, and many others. A friend was electrocuted, and as a result lost much of the use of his extremities. After a long bout of depression, he emerged to start a business making wooden craft items. He cuts out the figures with a saw, assembles them, and then his wife paints them. He again has a purpose.

How Can You Minister to Shut-ins?

Try to discern what the shut-ins need most, then act on your discovery. Do they need you just to sit and share conversation or do they need you to help with practical matters? Maybe they need a little of both. Consider the following ideas:

Make frequent short visits. One twenty-minute visit per week can be much more helpful than an hour visit once a month. While spontaneous visits can be fun, it is better to have a regular set time that the shut-in expects you. This way the shut-in can look forward with happy anticipation and can have any needs ready to share with you.

Supplement visits with phone calls and cheery notes. Send a colorful postcard when you go away on vacation. It takes only five minutes to let them know you think about them, even when you are not with them.

Remember the objective of your visit. If it is to visit with the shut-in, then don't spend your time visiting with other friends or family members who may be present.

Bring the outside in to them. Rearrange furniture so that they get a view of the out-of-doors. Decorate the walls with pretty pictures of nature. Lighten the room with new paint or accessories.

Each time I visited a young quadriplegic, I noticed a new travel poster on his wall. When I asked about them, he told me that his doctor gives them to him.

Always remember that you are a guest in their home.

Follow through with anything that you say you will do. Be careful of promising more than you can deliver.

Always try to take something with you. Ideas might include

I don't feel so good myself.

a flower from your garden, one of your children's or grandchildren's drawings, food or special treats like cookies or ice cream, cosmetic samples that you can get from the cosmetic department at a department store, church bulletin, magazines, books, tapes, or records from the library.

Take children with you occasionally. They have a way of livening up the conversation.

Avoid getting involved in family disputes and arguments. It's too easy to lose objectivity and thus lose your power as an objective sounding board.

Practice unhurried listening. If the shut-in is alone much of the time, they may tend to "talk your leg off." Have them tell you about happier times. Perhaps go through old picture albums and have them tell you about the different people in their lives.

Be cheerful. Smile.

Keep up with the latest information available on their illness or condition. Taking time to learn about the person's condition shows a lot of concern on your part.

Be generous with your hugs. There's power in your touch.

Offer rides to the doctor's office.

Compile a list of businesses that deliver—pharmacies, grocery stores, restaurants, and so forth.

Gather a variety of catalogs that will enable them to shop at home for articles for themselves as well as gifts for others.

Put them in touch with other shut-ins who would benefit from mutual sharing. They might develop a friendship "on-line."

As for practical jobs, the list could be far longer than you could ever handle on your own. The shut-in may not have the financial resources to hire the work done. Get several people from the church together to share the work. Twice a month a crew could go in and do a general household cleaning including changing sheets, washing clothes, scrubbing bathrooms, vacuuming, dusting, and so forth. There are tasks a teenager could come along to do like mowing the lawn and trimming the shrubs. With everyone working as a team, the time spent by individuals could be minimal.

Because shut-ins are usually looking at long-term care, it will be important for you as a visitor to pace yourself.

Should you overcommit, crash, and burn, you will be of help to no one. Remember the story of the sure and steady tortoise. Be a friend over the long haul, and your efforts will be more greatly appreciated.

Prayer for the Shut-in

When light is disguised by darkness and goodness is
   disguised as evil,
When the infinite capacity of the heart is disguised as
   the finite mind,
When the wellness of the soul is disguised by the
   body's infirmities,
When everlasting life is disguised in the paradox of
   crucifixion,
When immortality is disguised by that which is mortal,
When your presence is disguised in solitude,
Grant, dear God, that I might comprehend your perfect
   work.

When your boundless creation is disguised by form,
When your eternal love is disguised by longing,
When your undying compassion is disguised as indif-
   ference,
When your liberty is disguised in limitation,
When your mercy is disguised by injury,
When your salvation is disguised by loss,
Grant, my Lord, that I might comprehend your full-
   ness.

Oh, Holy Spirit, grant that by your heavenly presence
   in me
I might also comprehend your transcendence,
That on this path ashes will be transformed into beauty,
   mourning into the oil of joy,
   the spirit of heaviness into the garment of praise.

Amen.

                              DR. PATRICK O. THORNTON

4

Visiting in Nursing Homes

There is no known cure for old age (Chaplain LOWELL B. GRAVES).

Visiting in nursing homes is probably the most challenging, the most dreaded, the most rewarding, and the most neglected area of visitation.

Challenging because it is sometimes difficult to think of new things to say. It's difficult to talk with someone who can't hear. It's boring to listen to the same old stories again and again.

Dreaded because it reminds the visitor that growing old can be difficult. Nursing-home residents wish they could be in their own homes, and that is hard to hear.

Rewarding because residents gain so much joy over such little things. Rewarding because there is so much to learn from these experienced people who have so much to share, if only asked.

Neglected because there's not enough time, because we can't do anything to help their situation, because it is depressing to see people just sitting around waiting to die.

Unlike hospitals, where most people get better and are able to return home, nursing-home residents generally leave only when they die. One study in nursing homes revealed that the overt suicide rate is 15.8 per 100,000 residents. Overall, elderly Americans have 50 percent higher suicide rates than the general population and represent the group most at risk for suicide.

The elderly as a whole fear a loss of independence and of being a burden to others more than they fear death. Having to depend on someone else for basic needs, after having lived a life as an independent adult for many years, is humiliating and frustrating. Suddenly they find themselves being treated like children—and not very responsible children at that.

Following extensive research, Dan G. Blazer, in *Depression in Later Life* (Mosby, 1982), suggested that 30-50 percent of all nursing-home residents suffered from depression, thus making them at a higher risk for suicide.

A 1989 study of nursing-home residents revealed some very important information for those who visit with or have loved ones in these institutions. One hundred fifty residents in forty-five nursing homes in five different states were asked to rate the importance of choices in various aspects of nursing-home life. Results of the research showed that the most important factor to the majority of residents was being able to go out—to leave the home to go for a walk, to lunch, to shop, and so forth. The second was contact with family and friends through use of the telephone and mail. (A survey showed that 50 percent of nursing home residents do not get Christmas cards and 50 percent do not get visits from individuals.) The rest of the list, in order of importance, was having a choice of room-mates, personal-care routines such as bathing, recreational, entertainment, craft activities, mealtimes, and type of food, access to and control of their money, getting up when and if they wanted to, going to bed when they choose to, and finally, having a say over which guests come and when they come.

The foremost desire of seniors in nursing homes is to maintain their autonomy in the institutional setting. Taken along with the other findings of this survey, the visitor is given fairly clear guidelines within which to work.

But . . .

Let's overcome the objections to the visit in the first place. Then we can explore all of the possibilities that exist for a positive visit for both the resident and the visitor.

Lack of time. One woman told me, "Everyone is too busy. They don't have time with working and children and all to come to see me." Visiting a nursing-home resident need not and should not take large blocks of your time. Frequent short visits are more desirable than infrequent long visits. Scheduling a ten-minute visit between errands or other appointments can be sufficient without adding another project to your already long list. Will you be near by? Stop in for a quick visit.

Not knowing what to talk about. It doesn't take much to get a conversation going. Tell them about mutual friends and relatives. Share a letter or picture you received. Tell them about an article you read, a new recipe you tried, the tomato worms in the garden. It doesn't really matter. Ask for advice—remember they have years of experience on which to draw. Not knowing what to say is more of a problem in our minds than in reality. And again, let silence be your friend. If you are comfortable being there, the person you are visiting will tell you what's important to them.

It's depressing. Lack of short- and long-term goals goes hand in hand with loss of hope. There seems to be nothing to look forward to and nothing to live for. It is hard to see people grow old, feeble and unable to do much for themselves. It's really difficult when the person you go to visit doesn't even know who you are anymore. The challenge is, how can you make it less depressing for yourself as well as others?

First of all, you need to consider whose needs you are going to serve—yours or theirs. Your needs might be better served on a beach in Hawaii, but as bearers of Christ's love and concern, spending time with elderly persons may be just what they need to feel better.

Many visitors stop going because the resident doesn't recognize them or doesn't remember that they were there. Examine the purpose for your visit in the first place. What difference does it make to the person you are visiting? They will benefit from your visit because you are showing that you still value them as a person. They are still important because someone came to see them—whether or not they know that someone.

So, go ahead, *make their day.* The joy they experience and the gratitude they show will disperse the depression.

Making the Positive Visit

Here are a list of ideas for your consideration when visiting a resident in the nursing home. Many are based on the study mentioned earlier and others from interviews with residents.

1. *Call first or have a regular standing appointment.* In keeping with the principle of returning as much control to the resident as possible, ask when is most convenient for them. They may have other activities that they can enjoy and would rather visit with you when times are slow.

2. *Pray before you go.* Pray for a good visit with specific requests like Sally will know who you are, or that it won't bother you if she doesn't or that she will feel well enough to take a walk. Let them know that you remember them in prayer

3. *Touch.* Old people in general don't seem to get enough hugs. Be very liberal with kisses and hugs and hand hold-

ing. They desperately need the warmth of another person through physical contact. Other than the most perfunctory touch from nurses and aides in the routine of things, this may be the only friendly touch they get.

4. *Take children.* Young children are not as intimidated as adults. They give their love and affection more freely. Seldom is there a lapse in conversation with a young one around.

5. *Visit during non-holiday times.* While it is true that some people don't even get visitors during special days, the community and churches in general tend to provide more activities during the major holiday periods. Choirs perform. Services are conducted. There is more activity in general. While it is important to remember these times, visit in-between, too.

6. *Take something.* A cartoon, a flower from your yard, a picture of the kids, an ice-cream cone, a candy bar, the church bulletin, a child's drawing—all can offer a boost. It need not be a gift as such, but just a little token of your affection to let them know how important they are.

7. *Dress brightly and cheerfully and top it off with a big smile.* When I wear bright colors, even the most ill residents make comments.

8. *Speak to those who are sitting in the hall or lounge area.* A pleasant "Hello" and "How are you today?" can really brighten someone's day. Try not to walk past without at least a smile or some other type of acknowledgment to the other residents.

9. *If they have their own phone, call in between visits.* Let them know you were thinking about them. You might ask if they want you to bring anything next time you come. Mostly just make brief contact with them.

10. *Bring stationery and take dictation.* When I visited my grandfather, he always wanted me to write letters to his friends for him because his hand had become too shaky and his eyesight too poor. He dictated while I wrote.

11. *Take a camera along and take pictures of the resident and friends,* especially if there is going to be a special activity going on. They will enjoy passing the photos around to share with others and can mail them to those who live out-of-town. Get permission from the staff first as there may be some confidentiality issues involved.

12. *Give a simple party for a special occasion.* A bunch of balloons, a cupcake with a candle, and a small gift can make a birthday special.

13. *Send postcards or notes on pretty paper between visits.* Again, it can be as simple as "Hello, I'm thinking of you today. Can't wait to see you next Thursday. With love."

14. *If the room needs straightening, ask the resident's permission and then arrange it so that the person can manage more easily.* Keeping in line with the home rules and the resident's wishes, you might change the furniture around for a better view out the window, more light to read by, a more comfortable way to watch television, and so forth. How much you can do will be governed by the home in which the person resides.

15. *Where possible, have some of the resident's own things in the room.* A favorite pillow, blanket, nightstand, pictures, and so forth, gives the room a more comfortable feeling.

16. *Give the resident a manicure or pedicure that includes a massage to the hands and feet.* This is not only a good way to touch, but the nails will be a source of pride.

17. *Bring treats—with the okay of the nurse.* Fruit, milkshakes, sugarless candy, crackers. Go easy with the sweets.

It's been nice visiting with you, Grandma.

18. *Fix their hair.* All of us, men or women, feel better when we get our hair washed, styled, or just brushed. Again, this is a great way to touch.

19. *Ask yourself, "How would I like to be visited?"*

20. *If you can get permission from the home, bring an animal to visit.* The therapeutic value of having pets in institutional environments is documented. Some homes have a resident mascot or two that roam around receiving love and warmth from all of the residents. If the home you visit will not allow for a four-legged resident, perhaps they would consider your bringing a mellow pet out on the patio for

visits to the residents. The Society for the Prevention of Cruelty to Animals in Sacramento, California, and other cities has a wonderful program in which a volunteer takes a puppy or kitten to a local nursing home each week for the sole purpose of being cuddled by residents. Other animal protection groups do the same in other parts of the country. Consult the phone book for a listing of such organizations.

21. *Where possible, take them out.* (You will have to sign them out and gain permission from staff members.) It may only be for a short walk or wheelchair ride. Perhaps you could include them on a short shopping trip. Going out to lunch once a month might be a real treat, especially if you let them choose the restaurant. Selecting what they want off the menu can be very liberating after getting no choice in the nursing-home cafeteria. They may also appreciate your picking them up for church when they are able to go.

One man said that occasional trips outside of his quarters made a difference in his life and kept him from feeling like he was in prison.

22. *If you are a close family member, it is important that you help them preplan for impending deaths if asked to do so.* Again, you are giving the person control and inner peace knowing things will be just as planned. Talking about death is likely more difficult for you than for the elderly. It really is not a hard subject to address nor a hard conversation to begin. "John, have you ever thought about where you would like to be buried?" "Do you have any favorite songs?"

23. *Don't make commitments that you can't keep.* Nursing-home personnel will tell you about the "Sunday Glooms." Residents get up on Sunday morning and get all dressed up to wait for their visitors to come. It is heart breaking when no one shows up. If you say you are going to be there on a certain day, at a certain time, then be there. If

you can't make a specific date, then tell them you will come back as soon as you can.

24. *Listen to their stories over and over again.* Show interest in what they are saying. Ask them to elaborate. Ask questions. Show respect. Their pasts may be all they have. Certainly, the present is not where they would prefer to be, and there may be little hope for anything but worsening conditions for the future.

25. *Play board games or cards.* My grandfather loved to play checkers and dominoes. My grandmother liked Yahtzee. We spent many hours passing the time and sharing conversations over a game board.

Gift Ideas for Those in Nursing Homes

It is hard to think of suitable gifts for a friend or loved one in a nursing home. Home rules and regulations, as well as space available and security, can limit choices. Before you purchase a gift, it is best to check with the nurses to make sure it is acceptable. The following is a list of ideas. Add others as you think of them.

Basket of fresh fruit. Deliver with a bright bow and card attached. It is best to have the fruit in various stages of ripeness so that it does not have to be eaten within a few days.

Jams and jellies. My grandfather loved to take the home-made jellies down to the dining hall at breakfast to share with his tablemates.

Large print books and magazines. Reader's Digest is one of the prime publishers of the large print books. Your denomination may also have a devotional magazine in large print.

Audio tapes. There are a variety of musical tapes to fit

every taste. There are more and more books being put on tape and are available at local libraries. Many churches tape their sermons. Simple tape players are very reasonable to purchase. Cassette players allow patients to hear from family and friends who live far away and cannot visit. It is an opportunity for them to send messages not only of news but encouragement and prayer. Grandchildren can be included on the tape, perhaps singing a song or reciting a poem, as well as talking about what they are doing in school. Such cassettes can be played over and over and are a real tie with the world outside the nursing home.

Radio and cassette players with head phones are inexpensive and the volume can be adjusted to any level without disturbing others around them.

Pictures of family and friends perhaps in a pretty frame.

A photo album in which to keep snapshots and postcards.

Garments, preferably in their favorite colors. Smocks for women that open in the front with snaps are the easiest to get in and out of. There are men's shirts also that have snap openings. Consider slippers that allow for swelling feet. Extremities tend to have poor circulation and get cold easily, so make sure the slippers are soft and warm. There are some washable ones made of down that are very warm. Cardigan sweaters and lap covers are great for that little extra warmth needed. Robes for summer and winter come in handy. Women's slacks that have all elastic waists are much easier to slip on and more comfortable. There are men's pants being made that have velcro openings that make it very easy for arthritic hands to manage. Also consider hats and sunglasses to wear on out-of-door walks.

Magnifying glass. Some come with a light attached which makes it much easier to read. Try to get one with as large a lens as possible.

Address book. Fill it in with the addresses and phone numbers of people they want to write or call. Be sure to print large.

Hire a beautician to come in to do hair and nails. Many homes have beauticians available. Ask someone on the staff.

Bulletin board for the wall where the resident can display pictures, cards, and so forth that people send. Check house rules before purchasing and mounting.

Where applicable, the patient's own telephone, television, radio, clock.

Cosmetics. Men and women alike enjoy looking and smelling nice.

Inexpensive jewelry such as earrings, beads, a bolo tie make a person feel dressed up.

Lamb's wool, rubber rings, soft pillows for sitting may enable the patient to sit up longer in chairs.

Jigsaw puzzles. In one nursing home I visited, there was always a puzzle on a table in the lounge area. Residents would stroll by, fit a piece in, and go about their business. With everyone contributing, it took them about two weeks per puzzle. Make sure the pieces are not too small for old or arthritic fingers. There are some beautiful Norman Rockwell paintings that have been made into puzzles by the Milton Bradley Company.

Flowers are always a cheerful addition to any room. Think about live plants that the resident can nurture and watch grow. How about a flower pot, some potting soil, and some seeds?

Video tapes. The Long Beach (California) Memorial

Nursing Home uses video tapes to supplement personal visits. If the home has a VHS machine, make a family tape for your loved one. Or, you could have all of the old family home movies transferred to video tape. The old classics are on tape now; you might buy one that the resident especially likes.

New game equipment or board games for the recreation room could be shared by all of the residents. Talk with the activity director to see if there are any special needs. Playing cards that have very large numbers on them are available at most toy stores.

Funny little toys or anything else that will give them a laugh.

A bird feeder or delicate wind chime outside the patient's window. Be sure to bring an occasional supply of bird seed.

Yarn and other supplies for knitting, crocheting, cross stitching, and so forth.

Many nursing-home residents are blind and these special people are not able to participate in some of the activities sighted residents can. This varies from state to state but "talking books" (including the machine) can be sent to the blind without charge. Talk to your local library about how to get this service. The "books" are sent directly to the patient who can choose from a wide selection of material. Many local libraries have books on cassettes and even old radio shows (such as "Jack Benny," "Amos 'n Andy," "Fibber McGee and Molly"). Many vision-handicapped appreciate a description of what he or she is wearing, the colors, style. The resident may like to "feel" the soft sweaters or slippers.

Whatever gift you choose, wrap it in bright paper (use tape sparingly) and stick a pretty bow on it. Deliver it in person with a big smile.

Be Persistent

Some nursing homes are better than others. Some provide activities while others provide a mere bed and food.

But even in the best, a resident can feel lonely and isolated without contact from the outside world.

The very first woman I ever visited taught me why I was there. When I walked into her room, she seemed quite far away. The nurse even said something to the effect that she was unaware of where she was or who was there. Looking into her face, I suspected that perhaps she had escaped in her mind to a better place and a better time.

I walked over to her and held her hand. Speaking her name, I told her who I was, and that I had come to visit with her. She looked at me, and the vacant eyes became twinkling diamonds. She smiled as best she could and spoke a few words. As I left, I told her I would be back. Her eyes filled with tears.

From then on, every time I walked into her room, her glazed look would turn to a beautiful smile. I'll never forget those blue eyes shining at me with love, warmth, and gratitude. No one can put a price of time or money on the times we spent together. As with most visiting, I gained much more than I gave.

Consider adopting a grandmother or grandfather in a nearby nursing home if you don't know someone already there. Make it a family project. Your children will be blessed by the experience. Talk to one of the attendants at the front desk of the home. Tell them what you would like to do. They will certainly know of someone who could benefit from your concern.

One young mother started a group with several of her friends. Once a week, they take their toddlers to the nursing-home lounge where the children interact with the residents. Everyone has a great time playing and laughing together. It is a win-win situation for all involved.

Many nursing homes have family support groups. Family members should be encouraged to join such groups and exchange information. It's good to know how other people handle the sometimes difficult visits—to know that others are "in the same boat."

Elderly people who have young friends are considered by their peers to be very fortunate. At the funeral of a dear eighty-seven-year-old friend, I heard one of her quilting partners comment, "She had so many young friends."

While visiting with one woman she told me, "Old people want to talk about what's wrong with them. I get bored with that. I already know what's wrong with me. It's nice to talk to someone young."

Make time in your schedule to show love and concern for this special group of people. They need your warmth and concern.

" . . . In the world you will have trouble. But take heart! I have overcome the world" (John 16:33).

A Nursing-Home Resident's Prayer

Dear God,

You are a God who is concerned about us.
You know about the joys and the sorrows of our daily lives.
When we get up in the morning, you are there.
Long before we open our eyes, you see into our lives.
From the beginning of mankind, you have been with us.

As I have grown older, the strength of your continuing presence is a blessing in my life.
I do not always like the many changes that are occurring in my life, but you have promised to always be with me, no matter what happens.
From this promise, I gain peace.
God, you have meant the world to me and I want to say thank you.

Amen.

CHAPLAIN LOWELL B. GRAVES

5

Visiting Children

There is always a very well child within that needs normal play and creative outlet, who likes to talk about friends and school (PEGGY GULSHEN—Art Therapist and Coordinator of Children's Bereavement Art Group).

When visiting with children, it is tempting for adults to "talk down to," (over the head of), or through the sick or injured child. Often, the visiting adult will talk to the parent about the child as if the child who is the patient weren't even in the room.

Hospitals are scary places for almost everyone, but can be especially frightening for children, whose feelings are intensified by strangers who do unfamiliar things to their bodies, and by their almost uncontrollable feelings of loss and abandonment. Because their knowledge and (in the case of small children) their vocabulary is limited, it is more difficult to explain what is going on.

Many hospitals are confronting the issue by having children visit the hospital before they are admitted. One surgery center has the child and the parents come in a few days before to meet the nurses and to see a video describing the surgery. The child and parents are then taken on a guided tour of the center by a clown, who tells the children exactly where they will be and what will happen. Children are encouraged to ask questions. They let the child choose the "flavor" of the anaesthetic to be given. At the end of the visit, the children are encouraged to bring their favorite stuffed animal with them when they return to the hospital. They go home with balloons and other souvenirs from their visit.

This is all very reassuring for the planned admission, but many children don't get this opportunity to be so well prepared.

Understanding Developmental Stages

While every child is unique and children mature at different ages, it is helpful to recognize the characteristics of the different developmental stages. How you talk to a child will depend much on the child's age.

Under 5. Children five and under take things literally. You've probably seen cartoons or read humorous quips that refer to this. When Jonathan's mother said all of the noise was making her "climb the walls," Jonathan inquired what kind of special shoes she would need to do that.

Children of this young age have a hard time with the concept of time. They live in the present and the future has little meaning for them. Even "this afternoon" needs to be brought down to "after you eat lunch."

The concept of death is better understood as it relates to the physical body and is best explained by the cessation of bodily functions. "When a body is dead, it doesn't breathe anymore. The eyes don't see. The ears don't hear. It can't talk or walk anymore."

Young children think in magical terms. "The handsome prince kissed Sleeping Beauty, and she woke up."

Ages 6–9. As children grow older, their interests widen to include people and things removed from their environment, integrating them with past experiences. They have a penchant for details and facts. They begin to ask *How* and *Why* questions. Although still self-centered, they become more social and begin to make close friends. Being accepted by the group becomes more important.

Up until the age of nine, children communicate through art or play. Beginning around age nine, the child's vocabulary develops rapidly. Definite interests take shape and form. Using their own past experiences and collection of limited facts, they begin to come up with conclusions on their own rather than relying on what adults tell them to be true. There will likely be some residual "magical thinking" that still creeps in from time to time.

Ages 10–12. Preadolescents prefer to do things with a "best friend" or in a group, rather than on their own. The sexes don't generally mix in their activities because of insecurity regarding changing body image and developing sexual identity.

In one of the most difficult ages, preadolescent children are trapped between being "too old" for childish behavior, "too young" for adult behavior. The confidence they once had in themselves seems to diminish. It can be a very confusing time as the child begins to exercise independence.

Ages 13–17. Adolescence is marked by the primary influence being moved away from the parent and transferred to peers. Adolescents need each other. Wanting to be accepted by others of the same age is the primary driving force of behavior. Self-esteem is often based on whether or not they find acceptance in others. Gangs form to find a group that is accepting. Concern for appearance in the form of clothes, hairstyle, makeup, and physical features are paramount. Boys and girls "discover" each other first in groups, then singling out one another.

Suggestions for Visiting with Children

By keeping the information about developmental levels in mind, there are several steps you can take to insure a successful visit with a young person who is ill or injured. Always be asking yourself, "If I were sick, what would be helpful? What would be a real 'bummer'?"

Be honest. Lying to children or making light of their condition can cause loss of trust in you. This doesn't mean you need to frighten the child. But if you are asked a direct question, give as simple and direct an explanation as possible. Once discovered, a lie can make the child insecure, confused, and angry. If you can't be believed about *this*, what else is there that can't be believed?

Don't whisper about the patient. The imagination can fantasize something far worse than what is actual if patients think you need to be secretive about their condition.

Bring a small arsenal of little toys, puppets, paper, and crayons for the under-nine set. Let them communicate through play. Their fears, hopes, and needs will often be revealed through these special times of sharing in play.

Read to them. Selection of the book depends on the age of the child, of course. Ask the librarian for advice. Ask the child what kind of stories he or she likes. Have the child elaborate on the story by asking open-ended questions. "What do you think Peter should have done?" "Have you ever felt that way?" "Can you think of a different ending?" This gives them a chance to express themselves and may produce some revealing insights.

Tell stories to each other. An easy way is to have the child draw a picture and tell you about it.

Don't put words in their mouths. This goes along with not assuming you know how they feel or what they want.

Give them time and respect enough to tell you what they feel.

Don't overwhelm them with information. Give them bits and pieces of information as they can absorb it. Of course, when the children are older, they will be able to take in more facts at one time.

Asking open-ended questions such as "How do you feel today?" or "What's going on today?" gives the child the opportunity to share how they feel about what is happening.

Explain facts in a way that the child can understand. Some hospitals use dolls to explain a procedure. You might draw simple diagrams or pictures or use plastic models, if available. Check for understanding by having the child explain it back to you. (Be sure you check with a member of the staff before you undertake this!)

It's okay not to have all of the answers. Admit that you just don't know. Or you can give your opinion, letting the child know that it is just *your* opinion. Then ask the patient for feedback.

It takes longer to build trust and rapport with a child. Repeated short visits will help create a foundation of familiarity and trust.

Sick people don't have a lot of energy to meet new people. Children especially will feel more comfortable around familiar faces. Don't be surprised if the child says, "Go away." This doesn't mean they are ungrateful for your visit. It has already served its purpose. Children are just more honest and direct. The older patient might have the same feeling but never honestly expresses it.

Visiting with children requires interaction. You will need to participate by playing or asking questions. Drawing pictures together can be very revealing.

You need to be totally open and in tune with what the child is communicating. Don't go in with your own agenda. Listen for cues and follow the lead of the child.

Short visits can be just as good as longer ones. Look for signs that they are growing tired or feeling badly. If they become restless or disinterested, it may be time to leave.

Provide opportunities for the patient to have contacts with peers. If visits are impossible, then cards and letters from classmates at school or church can be helpful. Bring in news from the child's outside world. Phone calls from (or audio and video tapes of) classmates can be fun.

Let children talk about their fears and frustrations without your showing shock or fear yourself. Young children have not yet learned to hide their feelings. Their honesty can sometimes be alarming to the loved one that is trying to "protect" them. Don't isolate them more by not being willing to acknowledge those feelings.

Don't negate their feelings. That is, don't patronize. Never say they shouldn't be afraid, or shouldn't feel a certain way. Be understanding.

Affirm their loss. If they feel sad, affirm it by saying, "I understand," or "I'd be sad if I had that."

Be especially sensitive to adolescents' self-image. Help them talk out the things that concern them about their appearance.

While providing simple, straight-forward answers to children's questions, don't "over answer," thus confusing them.

Humor is a great healer. Be creative and apply humor whenever possible. But, don't "kid" with children. Remember how literal they are.

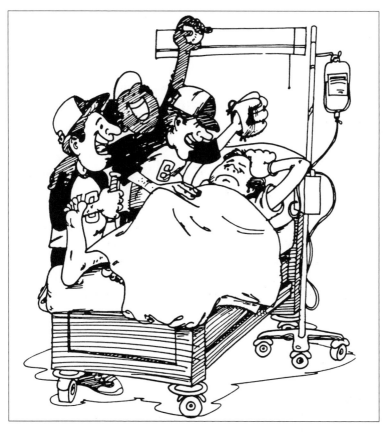

Don't worry about a thing, Ralph, the gang
is getting along just great without you.

Don't overprotect children. Instead, give them the tools they need to deal with life.

Visit with the child. Don't talk over the bed to the parents or others in the room. Go for coffee or tea if you want to minister to the adults.

Teenagers like visits from teenagers. Act as a taxi driver and bring a few to visit.

Children may regress (adults too) to immature behavior. They need lots of reassurance during this time. Give lots of hugs. Touch is important to children, too. Let them know that you are there and that you care.

Don't ever make children feel responsible for their illness. Children need to understand that bad things do happen to good people.

Children, like adults, feel more comfortable if they have some of their own "stuff" around them: familiar pictures, stuffed toys, blankets, and so forth.

Help them with homework. The more they can keep up with their schoolwork, the less they will have to face when they return to school. And it may help reduce one of their anxieties—that of falling behind their friends in school. Keep in mind, of course, their energy for being able to produce.

End the visit on a high note. Ask what you can bring the patient the next time you visit.

If it is too difficult or you can't be honest with children, then don't visit them. Children can really sense when you are uncomfortable or out of place. Send a gift or card instead.

Helping the Parents of the Sick Child

Validating and empowering the parents are probably the most important things you can do for the parent of a sick child. Let them talk about their fears and frustrations. You can affirm their loss as well. Parents are supposed to be able to protect their children and keep them safe. When those children get sick or injured, especially if it is a life-threatening situation, the parents feel guilt and inadequacy. Don't tell them they shouldn't feel that way. The fact is, they do. They need your support, your listening ear, your prayers.

Gather as much current information as you can on the injury or disease and *share the articles with the parents*. If they want to they will read them. This could help them to ask better questions of the medical staff. It can put some of their fears to rest. It can help them know the natural progression of the situation so that they will not be alarmed at changes.

Children need to receive any prognosis from their *parents*. Don't be willing to take on this role for them. Rather empower them through information, prayer, and encouragement to do the task themselves. Important information coming from any other person shatters trust in the parent and will distance parents from the child.

Offer respite, but don't feel hurt if they don't accept it. Parents need to get away for short periods of time to regroup and gather strength, especially if the child has long-term care ahead. Offer to stay with the child while they go. Help them find a place to get away. If you have access to a vacation facility, offer it to them. Again, don't be surprised if they graciously refuse to leave.

Take care of practical matters for them while they are attending the sick child. Maybe there are other children that need attention. Perhaps you could babysit, run errands, do some housekeeping, cook a meal, figure and check the bills for their payment, grocery shop, do laundry. Ask how you can help most effectively. By asking persistently and consistently, they may come to realize that you really *do* want to help.

There is so much to be learned from children. Their courage, their honesty, and their insight can teach even the wisest adult so much. Children are the teachers, if we take the time to listen.

A Child's Prayer

Our dear God, protect these sick and injured children. Give them the power to heal their wounds and to make them well. Protect them from evil and keep them safe. Care for their parents and keep them safe; for you have the power and the ability.

Amen.

CARL J. CORBETT
Age 12

6

Visiting the Terminally Ill

Perhaps some of the hardest moments of friendships occur when medicine can not triumph over disease ("In Sickness and in Health," Coping, *Summer 1988).*

Although it has been said in a variety of ways that life is a terminal illness, few people live as if their days are numbered. It is too easy to get bogged down in the day-to-day affairs of life and to forget how to live. Suddenly, a person is brought to this grim reality when they receive a terminal prognosis from the physician.

Emotional Needs of the Dying Patient

To effectively help the terminally ill patient, it is helpful to understand the emotional stages these people pass through. It is curious that the terminal patient's grief before death is very similar to the grief experienced by the survivors after death. Elisabeth Kubler-Ross describes the five stages of grief in her book *On Death and Dying* (New York: Macmillan, 1969).

Denial. "They must have mixed my lab tests up with someone else's." "There must be a mistake of some kind." "The doctor misread the reports."
Anger. "Why does this have to be happening to me?" "Why now?" "I don't deserve this." "Where's God when you need him?" "I worked hard all of my life—for this!"
Bargaining. "I'll stop smoking if you heal me." "I'll become active in the church again if you just get me through this." "Give me ten more years to raise my children, and I'll do what ever you want me to." "I'll be a better father if you just give me another chance."
Depression. "I'll never feel good again." "I'll never see my grandchildren grow up." "I'll have to depend on others to take care of me the rest of my life." "This is going to take every penny I have managed to save."
Acceptance. "I'm not enjoying this, but I am at peace." "I have fought hard and the end is near." "I'm ready."

Unfortunately some patients die without ever having reached the last stage—Acceptance. What is more unfortunate is that the attitudes of the family and loved ones of the patient may have contributed to their never being able to find peace.

Because loved ones are going through their own stages of anticipatory grief, they may not always be in synchronization with the terminal patient. In other words, patient Susie may have moved out of the Denial stage and into Anger, while husband John is still saying, "There must be a mistake."

One patient greeted me with relief as I walked into her room, "I'm so glad you are here. You are the only one that will let me talk about dying." She explained that every time she brought up the subject with her family, they would cut her off by saying she was going to be just fine and shouldn't talk about dying. Another patient said that the only one she could talk to about death was the cleaning woman.

When those around the patient are not in sync with the patient's stages, a very real distancing takes place. Because the patient already feels isolated, this can make for feelings of total desertion.

During your visits, you will probably be able to ascertain where the patient is after a few minutes of conversation. One caution to keep in mind: the stages are not like climbing a ladder. One doesn't necessarily go up one rung at a time. The lines between are not clearly drawn. The patient may fluctuate day to day—bargaining on Monday, accepting on Wednesday, and back to bargaining on Friday.

By understanding that these are stages that terminally ill people work through, you can better understand why they act the way they do on any certain day. A patient I'll call Janet learned that she had terminal cancer. On our first visit, she was very open. She couldn't believe what was happening. She thought it had only been the flu hanging on. We talked a long time about her prognosis. She wanted me to pray with her.

When Janet returned for chemotherapy two weeks later, her attitude was entirely different. She was angry with herself for smoking all of those years. She was angry at God for doing this, just as her children were raised and she could enjoy more freedom to be with her husband. I suspect that she was angry with me because I didn't have the answers for her. Janet was not at all open to prayer during this visit.

It is at this point that visitors often stop visiting. Either because they feel unappreciated or inadequate to do anything to help, they begin to distance themselves and find excuses for not coming around. Had I not recognized that what was happening to Janet was very normal and logical for her situation, I would likely have taken her coldness personally and would not have felt comfortable returning to visit.

It is critical that comforters of terminally ill persons keep offering support. The dying should never feel like you are giving up on them. Dr. Stephen E. Goldston, a psychologist with the National Institute of Mental Health says, ". . . the dying need to be dealt with honestly, without pretense, and safeguarded against the greatest pain of death, which is terrible loneliness."

Your foremost message to the dying person should be, "I am with you, and I am going to stay with you no matter what."

This may be easier for a pastoral visitor or friend than a family member. It is a natural form of self-preservation to distance oneself from someone you love who is dying. Somehow we think if we get prepared for it ahead of time, it won't hurt as much when it does happen. Those less invested can often be a great source of comfort just because they can listen and be more objective.

Besides keeping regular contact with the patient through visits, letters, cards, and phone calls, you can also help their emotional well-being by encouraging hope. This does not mean false hope that a cure will be found in time to save them, or that the tumor will miraculously shrink, or that an artificial organ can make them like new. Although all of these things are possible and all of us know of stories where miracles have taken place, it is more realistic to center on more attainable hopes.

The hopes of dying patients change. A college athlete may first hope to play basketball another season. Then his hopes change to living independently in his own apartment. Then to hoping that he can be out of the hospital by the holidays. Finally he may hope that his death is painless.

As comforters you can pray for and support patients with their hopes. Be careful that you move with them on this ever-changing journey. It is not helpful to encourage them to cling to yesterday's hope, or to push them too quickly into surrendering a hope they aren't ready to let go of yet.

Lack of information is one of the primary causes of anxiety among terminally ill. While you should gather as much current information as you can concerning their treatment and prognosis, it is up to their doctors to inform them. You can then help them form realistic expectations, when and if they are ready to face the reality. Support them in asking important questions of their doctor that they might otherwise forget or be reluctant to ask.

You can also assist the terminally ill by helping them live until they die. In the movie *Leap of Faith* the husband of the character who was dying became very frustrated with his wife's giving up. After having found her lying on the floor, paralyzed by her fear and depression, he made the statement, "You just lie around and wait to die."

"Make Today Count" is a national support group which believes every dying day is important. Carol Amen, author of the story which inspired the television movie *Testament*, fought a long hard battle with cancer. Up until days before her death, she was still writing and teaching. Determined to make every moment count, she had a huge celebration right before her death and invited all of her friends and family to a "She Lived Until She Died" party in her honor. It was a wonderful event.

What can *you* do to make today count for a dying patient? How can *you* support them in their efforts? The best way to find out is to *ask*. What is it that they always wanted to do? How do they want to leave this earthly home? How do they want to be remembered?

Answers to questions like these should give you a place to start. Come up with a plan together and encourage the patient to follow through on its implementation.

Emotional needs can best be met when you give the dying patient the message, "You can trust me with your feelings." Be open to hearing about their fear, guilt, and anger. Don't be judgmental either through words or body language.

One of the major problems dying folks have is the lack of open communication within their families. You don't know how many more chances you are going to get to share these intimate emotions, so don't delay.

Be careful not to change the subject when they want to talk about dying. And don't worry about what to say. Listen, touch, and feel with them. Share your feelings of helplessness and of love and concern. Admit that you don't understand. Acknowledge that you are hurting. Say that you feel helpless. Tell them you feel guilty for being so healthy. Confide your own fears about getting cancer or heart disease or whatever the patient suffers from. These feelings are normal. Sharing them can deepen your friendship. Be honest.

Even though people are dying, they need to be treated normally. Be yourself and remember that there is still within that decaying body a personality that you were attracted to before the illness.

Many patients suffer a loss of dignity as death progresses. Give them support by helping them to reflect on their uniqueness and special qualities and remind them that their feelings of worth are not limited to their present abilities.

As the time gets closer, the dying patient may need permission to let go. "We will be okay" can be great assurance for someone who is worried about the family. By doing this, we can let the patient die with inner peace.

Finally, say good-bye. Dying patients need completion. Put aside how difficult this will be for you and think first about the patient's needs. You will discover it is a precious and beautiful time, not morbid. Don't be afraid to ask if the patient has anything they need to say, any unfinished business. This can be a time to heal very old and deep wounds.

Practical Needs

Visitors can often help alleviate the practical burdens weighing on the terminal patients, particularly those who have no family. Such patients may need help getting their affairs in order before death occurs. Seek out professionals such as an attorney, tax preparer, funeral director, estate planner, and any others who can help the patients complete their business.

There are books and pamphlets on wills, probate, and trusts that may help them make some decisions. Help them gather all of the documentation that will be needed by the survivors to apply for benefits. The Social Security documentation requirements are a good guideline for your list.

The hospice philosophy has always been to return as much control to the patient as possible. Patients are

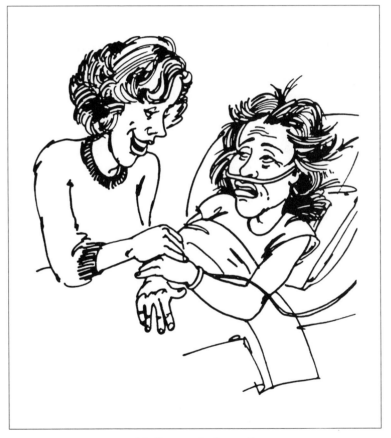

Martha, you look great!

encouraged to participate in their treatment. Encourage them to take control of the situations that are left for them to decide on such as "Living Wills." (A "Living Will" is the generic name for a legal document that expresses the individual's desires concerning personal medical care. If the person does not want extraordinary steps taken to prolong life, it can be so stated in this document. It is important that an attorney or physician be consulted to obtain the proper document for the state of residence. These documents must be properly completed in accordance with state laws to be valid.)

You may be able to help with the everyday housekeeping tasks or yardwork. As with shut-ins, this would be a good time to mobilize a task force to help with cleaning and running errands. When the work is divided, no one feels over-burdened. The patient will be relieved that these mundane chores have been attended to.

Put your patient in touch with national and community resources that can act as moral support and provide educational materials. There are thousands of support groups for just about every type of illness. These organizations will be a great benefit to the survivors of the terminal patient as well. See Appendix 2 for a partial listing.

Be flexible so that you can be there for the person no matter what the time of day or night. Rearrange your schedule to accommodate the dying. They need you *now*, while they are living.

If there are children still in the home, give them some extra attention. If possible, assign a special caregiver to the children, one they can count on for genuine empathy as well as for some fun activities to break the ever-present tension. Find out what the children need, and this may take some time if you are not close to them. Be aware of their grief and perhaps their inability to express it.

Don't keep children away from dying loved ones. They need to be close with immediate family members during this period. People often put unrealistic expectations on children in a crisis situation. They may be expected to do more work, do with less chauffeuring, or give up certain activities. Children may become resentful of all these imposed changes and begin to misbehave, become depressed, become overclinging to the sick parent, or any number of other reactions. They need to spend some one-on-one time with a trusted confidant.

Relationship Needs

Although I have never heard people on their death beds saying they wish they had spent more time at the office, I have heard many lament over failed relationships.

Resolving old conflicts and maintaining existing relationships are the primary goals. Both are necessary for the peaceful leaving of the dying patient.

Healed relationships are not only important for the dying person, but also for the survivors who remain to carry the burden of unfinished business. Two brothers who had contrasting values and lifestyles drifted apart to the point that they were barely speaking. One brother finally wrote a letter to the other asking that they get together and try to resolve their differences. The brother did not respond. His pride got in the way. Two weeks later, the brother who had written the letter drowned in a fishing accident. The surviving brother lives with the guilt and the knowledge that when an open hand was extended to him, he clinched his fist and drew back.

Grief counselors will tell you that the biggest roadblock to moving through and recovering from grief remains the "things left unsaid and undone." The young wife never got to apologize for being angry that morning. The father never told his son how proud he was of him. The brother never told his sister he loved her.

From the patient's point of view, this is unfinished business that needs completion. It's more than just "dying with a clean conscience." It's taking the bits and pieces of life and forming them into a whole—finishing the tapestry, writing the last line, reading the book to its end.

As a visitor you might have to risk rejection if you get involved in trying to heal relationships. Everyone will not be willing to "bury the hatchet." If those who are not are the survivors, they will be left to deal with it.

But there are steps that can be taken for the dying patient, even though others may not be willing to participate. Encourage patients to write what they need to say to someone in a letter. They can dictate to you if they are unable to write for themselves. Or, bring a cassette recorder and a supply of tapes so that messages can be recorded. Assure the patient that you will see to it that the right people get the letters and tapes.

Pray with the patient, if given permission, for the softening of hearts and forgiveness. Pray for healing of old wounds.

Reassure dying patients that they have done all that is possible, and that God will bless those efforts. Discuss how people are not always ready to receive the message we have to give, but often the time comes later. Jesus himself encountered such circumstances during his earthly ministry.

Concerning the maintenance of existing relationships, be certain first that you maintain your own ties to the patient. Be steadfast in your regular supportive contacts. It is not uncommon for friends to abandon dying patients. Watching someone die brings to the surface our own mortality and the fears associated with it.

Robert Stromberg points out that "friendships can become more highly valued or a source of disappointment when they do not provide the support expected." It's difficult to sit and talk with someone you care about who is dying, but don't let the fact that you feel helpless keep you away. Being alone and deserted is a real fear for the dying and they need your presence.

Cancer patients, whether terminal or not, often report cases of social rejection or isolation from even close friends. Betty Satterwhite Stevenson tells how in the supermarket, acquaintances would turn their carts around and go the other direction to avoid having to speak to her.

Do your part to relieve the fears and anxieties of the friends of dying patients. Educate them about what the patient is experiencing and how they can be of help. People often want specific tasks that they can perform. Help the patient come up with a list so that friends can have guidelines.

It may be that you can help by making phone calls to old friends who need to know of the patient's condition. Perhaps you would be willing to arrange hospitality for anyone who comes to visit from out of town.

Spiritual Needs

In the *Hospice Resource Manual for Local Churches* (New York: Pilgrim Press) edited by John W. Abbott, it states that the "Church is responsible for whether its members are prepared to die and for how they die."

By "Church," it is meant the caring and concerned members of the church family.

Warning was given earlier about making the hospital room a mission field. Most people who are dying have had ample opportunity for receiving the message of God's saving grace. Up to this point, they have either chosen to accept or reject the Good News.

Dying patients have the right to set the timetable for when they are ready to talk about their salvation. Your job is to be available for discussion.

One of my friends had a very serious disease. It finally progressed to the point where he had to be moved into the intensive care unit. We had visited many times. I always told him that I was praying for him and while he nodded acceptance, he never responded in any other way. When he was lying near death in ICU one morning, I sensed that something was very different. I took my cues from the patient, and followed God's little nudge and asked if he would like for me to pray openly with him right at that moment. He said yes.

Perhaps it was an answer to my private prayers.

Perhaps it was the sprouting of the seeds our visits had planted. Perhaps it was fear that the time was very near. Whatever the reason, the time was right just at this moment—not before, not later.

Ministering to spiritual needs includes looking at the person's fears, hopes, and expectations in the present sense as well as the future. It requires looking for the attachments they are holding on to, whether it is a person, place, thing, or circumstance. It might be a point of view that they feel they can't live without.

By helping the person verbalize the areas of their lives that are unsettled, we can either help them conclude the longing or help them redefine more realistically the problem and find satisfying solutions.

One chaplain gives an example. He was working with a woman who wanted to be present for her grandchildren as they grew up. Due to the nature of her illness, it was very unlikely. She felt a tremendous loss at their not ever knowing her. Together the chaplain and the patient came up with the idea of her compiling a scrapbook with pictures and articles about her life. She made tapes for them with stories and reminiscings. She wrote an autobiography of sorts. All of this helped her to face death, because it helped her to resolve a conflict within.

In chapter 1 we discussed the use of prayer and Scripture in ministering to spiritual needs. Take your cues from the patients and you will know when they are ready to accept these things. One patient made the statement, "I'm not sure whether or not I'm going to heaven. I've tried to lead a good life. How can I be sure?" This person was searching for answers. He wanted to know. He asked. He was ready to hear about God's plan of salvation.

Sometimes your cues will be more subtle. The person might say, "I've always tried to treat my fellowman right." This is a good opportunity for you to explore what the patient's beliefs are concerning salvation. Ask open-ended questions that will encourage longer answers. Cautiously lead into Scripture that can answer questions.

Leave a Bible nearby so that the person can easily

choose to turn to it. Highlight encouraging verses so that they can readily be spotted.

Sometimes the dying feel the need for confession. If you become the receiver of these confessions, offer encouragement by sharing Scripture that talks of God's forgiveness, God's love and mercy. Remind them of the happiness they have brought to others. Emphasize God's willingness and longing to forgive shortcomings. Use examples of how Jesus forgave sins of even harlots, murderers, and thieves.

The administering of sacraments or church ordinances is a religious rather than a spiritual function. But because they often go hand in hand, you might suggest their appropriate use and call the clergy if they want a particular service.

Never use phrases such as, "This must be God's will." "God doesn't give you more than you can bear." "God works in mysterious ways." "God must have a job for you in heaven." "You reap what you sow." "God would heal you if you had more faith."

These statements can be interpreted differently and are seldom encouraging.

Make Dying Easier

The dying are called on to do a lot of ministering to the people who come to visit them. It is often harder for the family to deal with the illness and crisis than the person who is the focus of the attention. Dying patients often feel guilty for having to make others grieve. They feel guilty for leaving loved ones alone. One woman's primary concern was over who would do the cooking for the family.

Patients often find themselves consoling the ones who will be left. They apologize for dying to anyone who will miss them.

They often have to hide their fears and appear cheerful when they are not, out of a sense of obligation to others.

That's a heavy burden to put on those who already have more than enough to deal with. Their energies are better used finishing old business, controlling pain, or just enjoying the time they have left in any way that they can.

Reassure patients that their loved ones will be okay. Tell them that they will look out for each other and grow as a result of the experience. Encourage them to turn their concerns over to God and have faith that God will keep his promises to be near always. Tell them that they are loved.

If you should be with the patient when death is imminent, and even if that person is unconscious, talk to him or her. Hold hands. The last senses to go are hearing and touch—that sense that someone is present. Use comforting words. Let the sufferer go; don't call him or her back. Reassure the patient that you will be okay. Give the dying a peaceful, quiet atmosphere in which to die. Stay for a while afterward if you like.

Jim Arnold in *Hospital Ministry* (New York: Crossroads, 1985) said, "God's presence is felt most vividly through persons who walk alongside." In whatever way you can, help them to die well.

When you have stayed with a dying person through the death itself, you will never be quite the same again; you will know something about spirituality. As one hospice worker put it, "At that moment of death, you know something has happened that is holy."

A Prayer for the Terminally Ill

God, we praise you for your faithfulness through life and through death. And as we sense the nearness of death the significance of your faithfulness deepens.

Entering the unknown is frightening and leaving our loved ones is hard. Wondering just how and when death will come is tedious.

Give us courage to face the challenges. Give us patience to endure the trials. Give us faith to overcome our fears. Give us guidance to reach the promised rest.

We ask these things in the name of Jesus.
Amen.

CHAPLAIN RON MULLES

7

Helping the
Primary Caregiver

Therefore encourage one another and build each other up . . .
(1 Thess. 5:11).

No book concerned with visiting the sick could be complete without some mention of those wonderful sacrificing souls known as the *primary caregivers*. These are the husbands and wives, sons and daughters, sisters and brothers, who tend the day-to-day needs of their loved ones.

The job, usually done for love, not pay, is draining. It puts restrictions on where the caregivers can go, how long they can stay, and even if they *can* go.

At Christmastime each year, California's *Sacramento Bee,* a local newspaper, sponsors a "Book of Dreams." The stories of different people in need are published in a special section. Readers are then invited to choose one of the people to help through contributions of money or goods. A few years ago one story appeared that struck the hearts of many, many people.

It was the story of an elderly man who had been the sole caregiver for his wife who had Alzheimer's disease. She had been in need of constant care for several years. His wish was to have the money to hire someone to come to care for his wife a couple of hours a week so that he could leave the house. His needs were simple: he just wanted to see people again. His dream was to be able to go down to the local shopping mall and just watch people go by for two hours a week. He felt that if he could do this, his life would be full. Community support came to his rescue.

Ways to help parents caring for sick children were discussed in chapter 5. Taking this further to include all caregivers, it is important that you comprehend the dynamics involved in caring for someone full time to understand how you may best serve these special people.

Primary caregivers often suffer burnout. The job can last for years. It's usually not very stimulating work, but rather involves physical stamina and tedious attention to details, such as keeping track of medication, constant cleaning to maintain personal hygiene, and preparing meals for special dietary needs.

Many times you see the elderly caring for the elderly. Instead of John and Martha enjoying their retirement years in travel and gardening, as they had saved for and planned, John is paralyzed from a stroke and Martha, a frail woman, has to take care of him. Like many spouses, Martha is really not physically up to the task, but out of loyalty, guilt, or financial considerations, her choices are limited. It is common to see primary caregivers hospitalized themselves after several months of having to care for someone else. They simply wear out.

Isolation, as shown in the example of the man who longed to sit in a shopping mall, is another major problem. As mentioned in the chapter on shut-ins, people tend to forget about long-term patients after the initial crisis is over. Along with the patient, the caregiver, too, is forgotten. Because such people are no longer sociably visible, people tend to call them to mind less often. Isolation is a real enemy.

Already alluded to, the physical demands on primary caregivers can be taxing. Often they have to lift the patient. They may have to assist in therapy. Necessary equipment can be heavy and awkward. Medications and monitoring may need to be done at all hours of the night, thus affording irregular sleeping patterns. Simple tasks can take hours to accomplish.

There can be financial strains. Frequent medical attention and loss of income because of illness can deal a great blow to even the best prepared.

Primary caregivers are often plagued with guilt feelings. They are torn between wanting to care for the patient and wishing they didn't have to. Sometimes they wish the person would just go ahead and die so that they can be free to lead a normal life again.

Emotionally the primary caregiver is often surrounded by a constant flow of negative thought. The job of keeping the patient's and one's own spirits up is demanding and often impossible. Maintaining hope that things will improve is a constant battle. Or, in the case where the situation is unlikely to improve, accepting that reality and living with it day after day is depressing.

If a sense of obligation is the strongest motivation, then feelings of being trapped may overwhelm the caregiver.

Depression can be the only steady companion. Depression is a result of grief. Grief is a result of loss. Depending on the circumstances, the patient may grieve over the loss of health, a job, ability to control basic bodily functions, fellowship with others, hopes and dreams, goals, independence. The list goes on and on.

Primary caregivers grieve for many of these same losses. Their dreams may also be dashed. Their social activities are curtailed and they miss friendships.

How Can You Help?

The three basic things you can do to help the primary caregiver involve *encouragement, relief, and validation.*

Encouragement. This can be shown through regular and frequent contact. Visits, cards, and phone calls that show you are holding the caregiver up in prayer are very helpful. Address your card and your message to the caregiver. Other cards should be sent to the patient. Address them as separate individuals, with separate needs. Make each feel special. To be most effective, don't make generic comments that cover both—personalize a thought to each. Pray with them if asked and always for them. Check your bookstore or library for books on encouragement that can give them hope and strength.

Be willing to take risks with your care-giving friends. Encourage them to ask for what they need from you.

Relief. This refers to the practical things you can do to help the caregiver. Meals are always a welcome relief. Someone else's cooking is such a treat after eating one's own cooking day after day. Running errands to the cleaners, grocers, pharmacy, or post office can be helpful for caregivers who cannot leave or are exhausted from a hard night. Providing a place of respite such as loan of your vacation cabin, your RV, or the spare room in your home as a place for caregivers to regroup is a very caring act.

One of the best ways to give relief is to sit with or care for the patient while the caregiver gets some time away. It could be for a few minutes or a few days. If you are in a position to provide this type of relief, strongly encourage the caregiver to accept your gracious offer. Be persistent, without being pushy, about caregivers needing some time off. If they refuse the first offer, make it again.

Validation. This lets the caregivers know that they are doing the right thing. Supporting difficult decisions by listening and being nonjudgmental is not only appropriate but also loving. Caregivers need an outlet to ventilate their feelings. For many caregivers, this is their first time at this awesome job. They think that there is a certain way people are supposed to die. They wonder if they are doing everything that is required.

Most helpful will be your listening for their underlying messages. Are they afraid? Let them know you will go through this with them. Are they experiencing guilt? Help them to forgive themselves. Teach them that one must accept forgiveness to receive it.

Listening is the key word. To hear, you need only your ears. To *listen*, you must involve the heart and mind. Advice and consultation may be appropriate if you are asked, but primarily, the caregiver needs an understanding ear. Isn't it curious that God created us with two ears and only one mouth?

Sorry, Bob, you're on a low calorie diet.

A Caregiver's Prayer

Gracious God, I confess how mixed my feelings are. I've got my health, and I should be grateful. But, why do I feel so empty sometimes? And, why do I feel resentment at helping? But, sometimes I do feel resentment. I just feel poured out, depleted, empty. God, help me accept my mixed feelings and most importantly, help me so that I don't inflict my pain on the one I most want to help.

Dear God, when I feel so tired and worn down, help me find the strength to carry on. And, save me from heroics. Help me put aside my pride and find the courage to ask for help. Oh, and thanks for the gift of life with all its pain, questions, mysteries. And thanks, too, for this life for which I am privileged to care, for this precious friend, mate, lover.

Amen.

REV. STEVE SMITH

8

The Church's Role in the Visiting Ministry

You are those who have stood by me in my trials (Luke 22:28).

The church is in a very important and unique position to support those in the congregation who want to participate in a visiting ministry. The vision for an orderly and organized visitation program geared toward those who are ill must come from the ministry. Without the recognition from and the constant encouragement of the clergy, the program will grow stale and weak.

Somehow along the way, the idea has come to be that only the professional clergy can effectively visit the sick. It is taken for granted that lay persons will take an ongoing part in the Sunday-school ministry, financial administration, and maintenance of the building and grounds. But members and clergy alike often feel that only the minister can correctly visit the sick.

Instead of being the "players," the clergy should instead be the "coaches" for the visiting team. Ministers should supervise the program. They should be there to develop a workable program, approach participants, and to commission them to do the work. When members are commissioned before the congregation in a public ceremony, everyone understands that a member of the visiting team, not the pastor, may be the one that comes to visit them.

The church needs to decide clearly that the visiting ministry is a function of the whole church, not just the clergy. Once this is established and accepted, the clergy needs to act as back-up support for those interested in becoming involved in this type of ministry.

Leadership Functions

The church can provide this leadership by instilling an attitude as well as establishing a workable program for its participants. To accomplish the goal of bringing together a viable visiting team, consider the following church functions:

Establishing a workable method for discovering needs. If the church is going to be a dynamic in the destiny of the world, then we as its members will have to go out to where the needs of the people are. The message of **Go** should be stronger than the message of **Come**. Christians need to seek out those who are hurting and need help. Coming alive to the needs of people and going out to them is one of the best, solid, evangelistic tools available to churches today. Churches can not grow unless they are out where people are, meeting human needs.

One doesn't have to go very far to find people who need help. Working with community services is one way. Listening for and encouraging members to share burdens is another. Unless solid, organized programs are established to take care of these circumstances, the whole program will quickly fall apart.

As far as the visiting ministry is concerned, the most

appropriate places to look for those who need visitation is through working with hospital chaplains, hospice, nursing homes, jails and prisons, shelters for the homeless, board and care homes—wherever folks who hurt are gathered together.

Making specific needs known. After the church has established a system for determining existing needs, the concerns must be passed on to the visiting team in an orderly fashion to avoid duplication of efforts, and to make sure that no one is overlooked.

Making the congregation sensitive and aware of visiting as a ministry through sermons and correspondence. The congregation needs to hear from the pulpit that people are literally dying from loneliness in nursing homes. Visiting needs to be considered as important as church attendance, tithing, and teaching Sunday school.

Providing training for the visitation team. There are at least two training series that have been established for this purpose. One is Ronald H. Sunderland's *Equipping Laypeople for Ministry* (P.O. Box 20392, Houston, TX 77225) and the other is the Stephen's Ministries series (1325 Boland, St. Louis, MO 63117). Both of these programs teach basic communication skills needed for effective visiting. Materials are well laid out and mainly require a facilitator to present the lessons.

Establishing a system of accountability. Those on a visiting team must be willing to accept supervision and be willing to share with a peer group. This system provides ongoing feeding and nurturing of volunteers. Without a time to share the tough visits, gain new insights, and learn from each other about how to develop skills, visiting becomes stale. When people don't want what you have to offer, it can become confusing. Visitors need a time and a place to debrief.

When you don't have to be accountable, you are more likely to miss a week—then two—and soon your visiting stops altogether.

Adopting special programs such as video-taped Sunday sermons for shut-ins and home communion for those who are unable to attend services. For children who are hospitalized for long periods of time, a Sunday-school lesson in the hospital or a time of reading children's Bible stories can remind the child that God is near.

These programs should be on a regularly scheduled basis so that patients and volunteers alike can depend on them.

Identifying and mobilizing support systems within the congregation and the community to meet needs. Information on resources needs to be constantly updated to maintain credibility.

Encouraging the youth of the church to become involved on a regular basis. Sunday-school classes could "adopt a grandmother" at a nearby nursing home. The children could make cards once a month and send to their adoptee. Once or twice a year they could have Sunday school at the nursing home, where the children can visit their "grandma" or "grandpa." The teacher could take pictures to exchange. The children could make simple gifts or bring flowers from home that the teacher could drop off occasionally. This same program could work just as effectively for shut-ins.

If there is a child in the hospital, the Sunday-school class might be encouraged to make cards, send a gift, make phone calls and visits if appropriate.

Teenagers can be involved in the visiting ministry. They could adopt a shut-in as their special project and donate time each month to do house cleaning and yard work. It is very important that teens learn to give without expecting anything in return. Youth ministering to the elderly can teach young people about life, aging, and death. Youth pastors can be vital in establishing a program.

Establishing ministries for those in nursing homes and shut-ins. This was discussed in chapter 3. These people need to be able to feel that they are still contributing members of the congregation whenever possible. There are jobs that they can do, even from their beds. They need to know that their work is important and needed. One lady, who is confined to a wheelchair, told me that her job was to follow up on anyone who visited the church the Sunday before. Someone brings her the slips that contain the information, and she calls and welcomes them and asks if they have any questions. Although unable to attend services, she is practicing her religion in a very vital way.

Another patient who was confined to her bed took her job as "prayer warrior" very seriously. She said that she had the time to pray for all of us who didn't have the time. Again, because her church and her family made it her specific job, she never felt very far away from her congregation.

Prayer chains are vital in any church, and almost anyone can be part of this ministry.

There are tape ministries in which elderly read Scripture or stories into cassette recorders for those who are blind or cannot read. A bed-ridden patient that likes to read may find this pleasurable.

A letter-writing ministry would work well for some. There are always those in the extended congregation such as missionaries, college students, and servicemen and women who would love to have a card or "care package" from the home church.

Licking stamps, addressing envelopes, folding letters, and stuffing envelopes may be things that some of your shut-ins can do.

There are those who could help others cope. A sharing network could be established so that these individuals could form support groups and friendships with others.

Some are just waiting to be asked. They would love to feel needed. Come up with some ideas and approach them.

Continuing to send weekly church bulletins, newsletters, and any correspondence to the nursing-home patients wherever they go. Mail is so important and regular contact from the church lets them know that they are remembered.

Sponsoring support groups for primary caregivers. In the January 1989 *Guideposts,* the story is told of Grove United Methodist Church in West Chester, Pennsylvania, where a couple who was taking care of an elderly parent started a group called Caretakers of Chester County. Its members are made up of primary caregivers. They have regular meetings and send out monthly newsletters and informational material to over a thousand members. The church provides a meeting place, financial aid, office resources, and congregational talents and leadership to the group. What a tremendous outreach!

Organizing regular church participation in nursing home services. In many communities various churches share the responsibility for special music and/or services on Sunday.

Without the shepherding of the leadership in the church, the sheep are apt to become discouraged and disorganized. Volunteer visitors must be given recognition and respect for the important role they will play in the outreach of the church.

Congregations should regularly hold them up in prayer.

Know Yourself

Visiting the sick is a special job. It requires patience and understanding and a love for what Jesus taught. It is a job that requires a lot of work. It is one that leaves the visitor with a richer appreciation for life and health. Like all ministries, you take away from the experience more than you give. The lessons are about love, courage, compassion, friendship, and commitment.

How involved you become in the visiting ministry will depend on your relationship with the sick person, your level of comfort, your abilities, and your interests. Sometimes being an effective visitor will mean modifying your behavior to suit the situation. If you still feel a bit apprehensive at this point, remember that like all other skills, it takes practice. The more visiting you do, the more comfortable you will feel.

Also be aware that no matter how at ease anyone feels with this ministry, there will be times when the visit doesn't go well. That is why the need for sharing and supervision is important.

It is important that you inventory your gifts and abilities and know where you fit in. If you cannot have a genuine concern for people, then there are other ways you can help. God gave each of us special gifts to use. Be honest with yourself, concentrate on the talents you have been given, and let those who have been given the personality to relate to others concentrate on this work. Some of us plant; others water; and some hoe.

Knowing your limitations is critical. I know one lady who is eager to drive folks to the doctor, cook for them, and clean their houses. But she can not assist them with their personal hygiene, sit and just listen, or be what she calls "nursey." These people are *doers*. They need a specific task. They can show God's love by running an errand, mowing a lawn, or babysitting.

Others are listeners. They can just sit and be present. They don't have to do anything.

Which kind of person are you? Where are your strengths and weaknesses? After you discover them, match your volunteering to your gifts.

In reaching out to those who are in crisis, people with both inclinations can be used to serve. Channeling your time and efforts in the appropriate direction is both a wise and an efficient use of time and talent. God will use others to fill in the areas where you can't serve.

Visiting the sick is a privilege. People often ask me how I do it. "Isn't it depressing?" they want to know. Those in an active visiting ministry never say their work is depressing.

The lessons to be learned about life and death are no better dealt with than in the room of a dying patient. We learn about strength and courage in the face of difficult times. We learn about the importance of sharing laughter when all else looks bleak. We learn how important our health is and we never take it for granted again. We learn about the importance of relationships and we begin to strive to keep them loving and intact. We learn what bonds people together—tears, laughter, prayer.

Visiting is a calling. And until the day comes that we can rejoice because there is no more visiting of sick to be done, we need to continue bearing one another's burdens.

A Prayer for the Church in Its Visiting Ministry

Father, you sent forth your Son saying, "Comfort ye, Comfort ye my people." Your Son sent us forth saying, "In as much as ye have cared for the least of my brethren, you have done so unto me."

Teach us to take your presence within our lives seriously. Teach us that when we walk beside those who would otherwise be alone, our feet leave your footprints. Teach us that you wish to touch with our fingertips, and use our voices to carry your comforting words.

Make us so that when in the presence of sorrow or need, we feel compassion well up within like deep waters seeking the surface of a dry land, aware that the fount of that well is your own searching love. You care within our caring. Now remind and encourage us to take that care into the lives of those who need it most.

Amen.

REV. CLIFFORD S. GRAVES

Appendix 1

Suggested Scripture Resources

Old Testament

Numbers

6:24–26	The LORD bless you and keep you.

Deuteronomy

31:8	Do not be afraid.
33:26, 27	God is your refuge.

Joshua

1:9	Be strong and courageous.

Psalm

16:8, 9	I will not be shaken.
22:9–11, 24	Do not be far from me.
23	The LORD is my shepherd.
27	The LORD is my light and my salvation.
31	In you, O LORD, I have taken refuge.
32:7	You are my hiding place.
34:4, 15, 17–19	I sought the LORD, and he answered me.
41	Blessed is he who has regard for the weak.
46	God is our refuge and strength.
55:4–8, 16, 17, 22	Fear and trembling have beset me.
56	Be merciful to me, O God.

57	Have mercy on me, O God.
62:1, 2, 5–8	My soul finds rest.
71	I will always have hope.
73:23–26	You hold me by my right hand.
77	I cried out to God for help.
86	Hear, O LORD, and answer me.
91	He is my refuge and my fortress.
107	Give thanks . . . for his love endures forever.
109:21, 22	Deliver me.
121	I lift up my eyes to the hills.
138	I will praise you, O LORD.
139	You have searched me and you know me.
143	O LORD, hear my prayer.

Isaiah

40:28–31	Strength to the weary.
41:10, 13	Do not fear, for I am with you.
43:2	I will be with you.

Lamentations

3:22–26	The LORD is my portion.

New Testament

Matthew

5:1–12	Blessed are the pure in heart.
6:25–34	Do not worry about your life.
11:28–30	Come to me, all you who are weary.
25:34–40	For I was sick and you looked after me.

John

11:25, 26	I am the resurrection and the life.
14:1–4, 27	Do not let your hearts be troubled.
16:33	In me you may have peace.

Romans

5:1–6	Suffering produces perseverance.
8:31–39	If God is for us, who can be against us?

2 Corinthians

1:3–11	Who comforts us in all our troubles.
4:8, 9, 16–18	Therefore we do not lose heart.

Philippians

4:6–8	Do not be anxious about anything.

Hebrews

4:16	Grace to help us in our time of need.
13:5	Never will I leave you.

1 Peter

5:7	Cast all your anxiety on him.

1 John

3:1, 19, 20	How great is the love.

Appendix 2

Support Groups for the Sick and Their Caregivers

Aging

Aging in America
1500 Pelham Parkway, S.
Bronx, NY 10461
(212) 824-4004

Children of Aging Parents
c/o Mirca Liberti
2761 Trenton Road
Levittown, PA 19056

Gerontological Society of America
1275 K Street, N.W., Suite 350
Washington, DC 20005-4006
(202) 842-1275

National Alliance of Senior
 Citizens
2525 Wilson Boulevard
Arlington, VA 22201
(703) 528-4380

Nursing Home Advisory and
 Research Council
P. O. Box 18820
Cleveland Heights, OH 44118
(216) 321-0403

AIDS

National AIDS Network
2033 M Street, N.W., Suite 800
Washington, DC 20036
(202) 293-2437

Rise n' Shine (babies and children)
910 Cobb Building
1305 Fourth Avenue
Seattle, WA 98101
(206) 628-8949

Alzheimer's Disease

Alzheimer's Disease and Related
 Disorders Association, Inc.
70 East Lake Street
Chicago, IL 60601
(312) 853-3060

Birth Defects

March of Dimes Birth Defects
 Foundation
1275 Mamaroneck Avenue
White Plains, NY 10605
(914) 428-7100

Burns

American Burn Association
c/o Shriners Burn Institute
202 Goodman Street
Cincinnati, OH 45219
(513) 751-3900

The Phoenix Society, Inc.
11 Rust Hill Road
Levittown, PA 19056
(215) 946-2876

Cancer

The American Cancer Society has many local support groups and organizations nationwide—I Can Cope, Can-Surmount, Reach to Recovery (mastectomy), International Association of Laryngectomees (IAL), United Ostomy Association (colostomy, ileostomy, urostomy surgery), Y-Me. Contact your local American Cancer Society for names and locations of meetings.

The American Cancer Society
1599 Clifton Road, N.E.
Atlanta, GA 30329
1 (800) ACS-2345

Cancer Care, Inc., and the
  National Cancer Care
  Foundation
1180 Avenue of the Americas
New York, NY 10036
(212) 221-3300

Cancer Family Care
7710 Reading Road, Suite 204
Cincinnati, OH 45237
(513) 821-3346
Answerline—information and
  referral for cancer (513) 821-9949

The Candlelighters Childhood
  Cancer Foundation
1312 18th Street, N.W., Suite 200
Washington, DC 20036
(202) 659-5136

Corporate Angel Network (provides air transportation to cancer
  treatment facilities)
Building 1, Westchester County
  Airport
White Plains, NY 10604
(914) 328-1313

The Leukemia Society of America
733 Third Avenue, 14th Floor
New York, NY 10017
(212) 573-8484

National Cancer Institute
9000 Rockvale Pike
Bethesda, MD 20892
(301) 496-4000

The National Coalition for Cancer
  Survivorship
323 Eighth Street, S.W.
Albuquerque, NM 87102
(505) 764-9956

United Cancer Council, Inc.
4010 W. 86th Street, Suite 8
Indianapolis, IN 46268
(317) 879-9900

Craniofacial Abnormalities

Let's Face It
P. O. Box 711
Concord, MA 01742
(508) 371-3186

National Craniofacial Foundation
3100 Carlisle, Suite 215
Dallas, TX 75204
(214) 871-1399

Cerebral Palsy

United Cerebral Palsy Association
66 E. 34th Street
New York, NY 10016
(212) 481-6300

Cystic Fibrosis

Cystic Fibrosis Foundation
6931 Arlington Road, No. 200
Bethesda, MD 20814
(301) 951-4422

Death of a Child

Centering Corporation (also hand-
  icapped infants)
P. O. Box 3367
Omaha, NE 68103
(402) 553-1200

The Compassionate Friends
P. O. Box 3696
Oak Brook, IL 60522-3696
(312) 990-0010

MADD (Mothers Against Drunk
  Driving)
669 Airport Freeway, Suite 310
Hurst, TX 76053
(817) 268-6233

Diabetes

American Diabetes Association
National Service Center
P. O. Box 25757
1660 Duke Street
Alexandria, VA 22313
(703) 549-1500

Juvenile Diabetes Foundation
  International
432 Park Avenue, S.
New York, NY 10016
(212) 889-7575

Epilepsy

American Epilepsy Society
c/o Priscilla S. Bourgeois
179 Allyn Street, No. 304
Hartford, CT 06103
(203) 246-6566

Epilepsy Foundation of America
4351 Garden City Drive
Landover, MD 20785
(301) 459-3700

Genetic Disorders

SOFT—Support Organization for
  Trisomy 18, 13 and other related
  disorders
2982 S. Union Street
Rochester, NY 14624
(716) 594-4621

Hearing/Speech Impairment

American Auditory Society
1966 Inwood Road
Dallas, TX 75235
(214) 905-3001

National Association of the Deaf
814 Thayer Avenue
Silver Springs, MD 20910
(301) 587-1788

Self-Help for Hard of Hearing
  People
7800 Wisconsin Avenue
Bethesda, MD 20814
(301) 657-2248

Heart Disease

American Heart Association
Mended Hearts
7320 Greenville Avenue
Dallas, TX 75231
(214) 373-6300

Kidney Disease

American Kidney Foundation
6110 Executive Boulevard, Suite
  1010
Rockville, MD 20852
(301) 881-3052

Lung Disease

American Lung Association
1740 Broadway
New York, NY 10019
(212) 315-8700

Lupus

Lupus Foundation of America
1717 Massachusetts Avenue, N.W.,
  Suite 203
Washington, DC 20036
(202) 328-4550

Multiple Sclerosis

National Multiple Sclerosis
  Society
205 E. 42nd Street
New York, NY 10017
(212) 986-3240

Muscular Dystrophy

Muscular Dystrophy Association
810 7th Avenue
New York, NY 10019
(212) 586-0808

Pain

American Pain Society
1200 17th Street, N.W., Suite 400
Washington, DC 20036
(202) 296-9200

Parkinson's Disease

American Parkinson's Disease
  Association
116 John Street, Suite 417
New York, NY 10038
(212) 732-9550

Parkinson's Educational Program
1800 Park Newport, No. 302
Newport Beach, CA 92660
(714) 640-0218

Sickle Cell Disease

National Association for Sickle
  Cell Disease
4221 Wilshire Boulevard, Suite 360
Los Angeles, CA 90010
(213) 936-7205

Spinal Cord Injury

National Spinal Cord Injury
  Association
600 W. Cummings Park, Suite
  2000
Woburn, MA 01801
(617) 935-2722

Stroke

National Stroke Association
300 E. Hampden Avenue, Suite
  240
Englewood, CO 80110-2622
(303) 762-9922

Suicide

Suicide Prevention Center, Inc.
P. O. Box 1393
Dayton, OH 45401
Business phone   (513) 223-9096
24-hour hotline   (513) 223-4777

Terminal Illness

Children's Hospice International
1101 King Street, Suite 131
Alexandria, VA 22314
(703) 684-0330

Make a Wish Foundation of
  America (provides last wishes
  for terminally ill children)
2600 N. Central Avenue, Suite 936
Phoenix, AZ 85004
(602) 240-6600

Make Today Count
101 1/2 South Union Street
Alexandria, VA 22314
(703) 548-9674

National Hospice Organization
1901 N. Moore Street, Suite 901
Arlington, VA 22209
(703) 243-5900

Visual Impairment

American Foundation for the
  Blind
15 W. 16th Street
New York, NY 10011
(212) 620-2000

Christian Record Services
4444 S. 52nd Street
Lincoln, NE 68516
(402) 488-0981